The Hidden Power of Undefeatable Faith

Lessons of Faith from the Life of Rizpah

GLENDA MALMIN

CITY BIBLE
PUBLISHING
Portland, Oregon, U.S.A.

The Hidden Power of Undefeatable Faith

"We are living in a time when God is sovereignly apprehending women for His purposes. Glenda Malmin does an outstanding job in helping women arise during this season for God's purpose for their lives. She reveals the power of God that can be released through any seemingly insignificant woman. However, no one is insignificant to God. Destiny awaits women who, like Rizpah, will answer the call to intercession. A new level of faith will position you for your destiny. After reading The Hidden Power of Undefeatable Faith, you will be forever changed! I highly recommend this book to those who are interested in achieving God's highest goals."

— *DR. BARBARA WENTROBLE* President and Founder
Wentroble Christian Ministries

"Glenda Malmin is an unusually gifted writer and communicator. She is producing a refreshing new genre of Christian resources that will set a new tone for a new generation. Read with joy!"

— *WENDELL SMITH* Senior Pastor
The City Church

The Hidden Power of Undefeatable Faith

"In The Hidden Power of Undefeatable Faith, Glenda Malmin uses her unique writing style of blending a story from scripture with insightful fictional narrative to skillfully weave a written tapestry of lessons of faith and encouragement. As the life story of Rizpah unfolds, I trust readers will delightfully discover (as I did) that faith is strengthened, hope is renewed, passion is restored, and purpose is revived. I challenge you to walk with Rizpah and become a person of Undefeatable Faith in your generation. With profound gratitude, I thank you, Glenda, for investing in our lives that we may all become 'hot coals on the tip of the Marksman's arrow.'"

— *BARBARA WRIGHT* Associate Pastor
The City Church

"As women, we often feel that it is feminine to be a little fearful! But in this book Glenda challenges us to boldly take hold of our destiny, and with new confidence pay the price to make it happen. After all ladies, you will never know unless you have a go!"

— *RACHEL HICKSON* Director
The Heartcry Ministry, London, UK

Published by City Bible Publishing
9200 NE Fremont, Portland, Oregon 97220
Printed in U.S.A.

City Bible Publishing is a ministry of City Bible Church and is dedicated to serving the local church and its leaders through the production and distribution of quality materials. It is our prayer that these materials, proven in the context of the local church, will equip leaders in exalting the Lord and extending His kingdom.

For a free catalog of additional resources from City Bible Publishing, please call 1-800-777-6057 or visit our web site at www.citybiblepublishing.com.

The Hidden Power of Undefeatable Faith
© Copyright 2004 by City Bible Publishing.   All Rights Reserved.

ISBN: 1-593830-18-1

Italics in Scripture are the author's emphasis.
Unless otherwise indicated, all Scripture quotations are from:

The Holy Bible, New King James Version (NKJV) © 1984 by Thomas Nelson, Inc.

Other Scripture quotations are from:

The Holy Bible, New International Version (NIV)
© 1973, 1984 by International Bible Society, used by permission of Zondervan Publishing House.

New American Standard Bible® (NASB) © 1960, 1977, 1995 by the Lockman Foundation. Used by permission.

The Holy Bible, King James Version (KJV)

The Living Bible (TLB)
© 1971. Used by permission of Tyndale House Publishers, Inc. All rights reserved.

The Message
© 1993, 1994, 1995, 1996, 2000, 2001, 2002. Used by permission of NavPress Publishing Group.

The New Testament in Modern English, Revised Edition (Phillips) © 1958, 1960, 1972 by J. B. Phillips.

Table of Contents

I would like to dedicate this book to two incredible women who have been a constant example to me of faith that is absolutely undefeatable. They have both faced numerous odds that would be insurmountable to many, but not to them.

To my wonderful mother-in-law, Leona Malmin, I say thank you. You have inspired and strengthened my faith for many years now; I am deeply indebted to you for your life example of unwavering faith. I stand in awe of your never-ending positive confession in the midst of the overwhelming trials that have been presented to you these many years.

To my mentor and friend, Edie Iverson, I am forever grateful for you. You are a true heroin of faith. I never cease to be amazed at your undeniably undefeatable faith for God's people. You are not only a teacher of faith in speech; you live and walk by it as well. Thank you for the many conversations of faith over the years, and for inviting me into a personal, close-up view of your life. Thanks for inviting me in; thank you for the years.

Acknowledgements

I give honor and thanks to my Lord and Savior, Jesus Christ, for giving me salvation as a precious and personal gift. Thank You for continuing your work of faith in me. Thank You for never wearying of my feeble attempts to exercise faith and for patiently working to develop a faith in me that is maturing while in the process of becoming absolutely undefeatable. I am forever grateful to You for the kindness and grace you have extended to me; what a patient and loving Savior You are. You are indeed worthy to be praised!

A genuine offering of thanks and honor goes to my husband, Ken. Thank you for your continual encouragement and sensitivity to the writing process. You always give me perspective, balance, and the faith to go forward. I have enjoyed our journey of faith together these past thirty-three years, and am looking forward to our future together as well.

I would like to thank my daughter Angie Prosser and my dear friend Mary Henderson for being my "1st look responders" to the original manuscript. Your responses of tears and always wanting the next chapter, as well as your faithful prayers were an inspiration to me in the journey and increased my faith daily. I love and appreciate you both. Thank you for your impartation of undefeatable faith to these pages. I pray that it will bless others in the way that you are both a blessing to me.

I would also like to thank my daughter-in-law Rebecca and my friend of many years, Donna Chesnutt for also reading the initial manuscript and encouraging me along the way. Your prayers and encouragement have meant more to me than words can really express. I am forever grateful to you both. I am also incredibly grateful to my other prayer partners, my parents, John and Trevah Casson, my parents-in-law, Leif and Leona Malmin, Phyllis Brown, Don and Kathy Ballantyne, Matt Rogers, Fred and Lynn Whaley, and Evind and Andrea Schweiss. Your faithful prayers have kept me steady in the midst of a busy schedule. I pray that this book will honor the hours of prayer that you have invested.

Thanks to Lanny Hubbard, Bo Malmin and Don Ballantyne for helping me with research for this project. Your assistance was a valuable asset to the work on these pages, and I greatly appreciate it. A sincere thank you to Rich Brott, Jason Prosser and Casey Corrigan for being my "faith stretchers" and encouragers in this process. You have challenged and encouraged me to live up to the faith that I proclaim in these pages.

Foreword

Glenda Malmin and I have shared a close personal friendship for many years, and I greatly admire and respect her as a godly woman and an awesome leader in the kingdom of God. She currently serves as Dean of Women at Portland Bible College, teaches both in the college and our local church, and travels extensively, speaking at women's retreats and conferences. This book is one more expression of Glenda's unique ability to glean principles from her diligent study of the Word and this particular story that most people would no doubt pass over and not even bother to research.

The journey of this insignificant woman named Rizpah will touch your heart as you become acquainted with her life of disappointment and personal tragedy. Glenda's book is not just for women, but for anyone who desires to cultivate a heart and spirit that causes you to face each new day with eyes of faith. Rizpah's story is one that teaches us that undefeatable faith is available to every person that will stand their ground in adversity and believe that God will reward their spirit of faith. Like most of us, Rizpah had gone through the trials of disappointment and hopelessness, only to rise to a new level of blessing and reward.

If you are feeling discouraged, finding yourself in one of life's deep valleys, perhaps facing an overwhelming obstacle or contradiction, if you have been taken advantage of or are seemingly forgotten, then this book is definitely for you. The principles of truth found here will help shape your hopes and dreams into those of an undefeatable individual, standing strong in the Lord to face whatever circumstances may come your way.

— SHARON DAMAZIO
City Bible Church, Portland, Oregon

Preface

Contradictions and personal tragedies come in all shapes and sizes. Some challenge your sense of humor and some your faith. Some are insignificant and some are life changing.

What is insurmountable to one may not be to another. Contradictions, disappointments, and tragedies come to all, in different ways and at different seasons of life. They can make or shake your confidence and strengthen or shatter your faith. All have an element of loss attached to them, and all have the potential to rob you of faith in a mighty and personal God who genuinely cares about your very personal world.

Over the course of human history, wars have resulted in a loss of national security; fires, floods, and tornadoes have stirred in the heart a sense of a lack of community security; and random shootings in schools and neighborhoods have created fear and a loss of personal security. Perhaps you have lost a family member to death or divorce, a friend to disease, a baby to miscarriage, a child to drugs on the streets of your city. Perhaps you have lost your job, your health, or your emotional stability. Regardless of the loss, whether it is national, within the community, or personal, to overcome you need a faith that is undefeatable.

Hebrews 11:1–2 says, "The fundamental fact of existence is that this trust in God, this faith, is the firm foundation under everything that makes life worth living. It's our handle on what we can't see. The act of faith is what distinguished our ancestors, set them above the crowd" (The Message).

Faith does not come by hoping; it comes by continuing to put one foot in the front of the other in the face of seeming unbeatable odds. It comes by pouring out your heart to God and letting Him pour back into you and then through you. It comes not by sheer will, but by faith in the One who can hold your hand in the storm and walk you to dry land. It is that act that "distinguished our ancestors, set them above the crowd" and will enable us to say to the subsequent generation, "Follow me as I follow Christ."

Are you willing to remain on the pathway of life and beat the unbeatable odds? Are you willing to trust in the One who made heaven and earth? Are you willing to keep your hand in the hand of Almighty God, regardless of what comes, as He leads you on the pathway of life,? Are you willing to trust Him when there is no one else to trust? If you are, then you have what it takes to be a person of undefeatable faith.

I'd like to tell you the story of an amazing woman of antiquity by the name of Rizpah. The story of her life as recorded in the Bible is short in verse but rich in meaning. As you read her story, I pray that you will see how her journey so intimately parallels your journey and the journey of so many people you know.

Rizpah's story will be different than yours, and yet the heart-issues and principles will ring true to your heart. She was a woman who had a hope and a desire to make a difference in her generation. She had a faith that was undefeatable, a faith that pierced the heart of a king and rescued a people from disaster. She was a woman whose hope was seemingly crushed, but because her feet were planted on the Rock, her story is still told today. Her life not only made a difference in her day, but it shoots across the generations and ministers "rains of refreshing" and hope to us today.

At the beginning of each chapter, you will find a brief quoted portion of Scripture from 2 Samuel. Then through story and mono-logue format, you will be introduced to Rizpah and the other characters of her story as though they were personally telling you a part of their own journey. Granted, a measure of poetic license is taken as the ponderings of their private heart-thoughts and prayerful petitions unfold in each chapter. Some parts of the narrative are fictional surmising, although very realistic in possibility. As the biblical characters come alive, you will find that their experiences hold many keys to aid you in your personal walk of undefeatable faith.

The primary focus of this book is not so much on exegetical interpretation as on the personal application of principles of truth in the quoted verses. I desire that you, the reader, would seek to apply the lessons drawn from the life of Rizpah. Let her life's story mark you for destiny. Let it shape you and mold you into the person of undefeatable faith that you desire to be. Let it encourage you to stand strong in the trial you are in today or you may face tomorrow. It is absolutely God's sovereign will for you, like Rizpah, to be a person of undefeatable faith, regardless of what circumstance comes your way.

First Corinthians 10:11 says, "Now all these things happened to them as examples, and they were written for our admonition, upon whom the ends of the ages have come." Rizpah's story was written for you and for me. Who will read your story, and what will they read in the pages of your life in the years to come? Let's be challenged together as we look at this amazing woman's life.

Section One

Faith's Call to Destiny

THE HIDDEN POWER OF UNDEFEATABLE FAITH

Perspectives of God and Man

History's Claim and Destiny's Call

And Saul had a concubine, whose name was Rizpah, the daughter of Aiah
— 2 Samuel 3:7

Desperately, he held tightly to the rope that could lift him to the trace of light at the top of the well, but to no avail his feet continued to slip down the muddy wall. As he quickly glanced downward, he could see no end to the darkness beneath him, and the light at the top eluded him. His footing began to give way to the muck and mire pasted to the well's circular wall, both representative of his life—an unending circle of muck and mire. The rope began to burn his cramped and now numb hands; he felt the weight of his body slip. In agony he grabbed the rope more tightly, all the while losing his grip. Now falling and kicking, he reached upward in a panicked frenzy while plummeting into the darkness of the bottomless pit below. Screaming out in paralyzing fear, he awakened himself with a start from this all-too-familiar nightmare.

Although these nightmares had become familiar and frequent, they were never expected and were always terrorizing. They left him drenched in sweat and shaking from the horror of the darkness that seemingly longed to swallow him.

Life had been long and hard for him, as it had been for his father before him and his father before him. He was born into a family plagued by the disappointment of reaching for the top but never attaining. Some days were filled with suffocating heaviness in his soul; he could tell that this would be one of those days. It was meant to be a day of great joy, but he could feel the nightmarish darkness of the well crawling up his legs; he recognized its oppressive presence. He knew disappointment was just around the corner. He could hear the echoes of taunting nipping at his heels. Even on a day filled with sunshine, he could see clouds of despair forming in the distance. He could feel the grayness of each day soaking into his mind, into his heart, into the very fiber of his being.

His own father had taken but one brief look at him on the day of his birth, and instead of rejoicing for the gift of a healthy son, he hastily prophesied his destiny by naming him Aiah, meaning "screeching hawk, vulture." [1] Doomed from the first day of his life, Aiah had always been a boy who walked with a slow, lifeless step and a whine in his voice. In fulfillment of the name his father had so expeditiously christened him with, Aiah screeched his way through life to get what he wanted. With each tribulation that life brought his way, he composed lamenting expressions and woeful complaints into somber lyrics in minor keys. "Woe is me!" was his personal theme song, and an overcast of gray was the unremitting backdrop of the chapters of his life.

Like the vulture he was named for, when Aiah didn't get what he wanted, he reached for what others had. He continually swindled his way through life, benefiting from the fruits of others' hard labor. Whether his lot in life was improving or not, complaints and negative confessions were his constant companions. They were his familiar friends; he didn't know how to think any other way.

Then he met and married his wife. Cloudless days and starlit nights were ahead, he was sure of it. His personal theme song apprehensively changed from minor keys to majors. His bride was beautiful to behold. With her raven black hair, flashing brown eyes, and coy smile, she had captured his heart and the hearts of many other young men in the neighborhood. Aiah's father was initially resistant to his son's request for this fair maiden's hand. Although he wanted grandsons, he thought the possibility of this match was remote, if at all possible. He didn't think that he, as Aiah's representative, would have a prayer's hope with her father in the betrothal bargaining process, but Aiah lamented to his father until he caved in, pocketed his pride, and made his approach.

Much to his surprise, the girl's father agreed and gave his daughter in marriage to Aiah. It was the happiest day of Aiah's life, not so much because he now had a bride, but because he could have a son. Only a son could bring to him a truly cloudless day. All his hopes rested in the possibility that God would grant him a son. After all, a man with no sons was no man at all—not in his neighborhood.

A year passed, then two, and then three. Finally, in the seventh year, the day had arrived. Today the pangs of labor had begun and the time of giving birth was now coming to Aiah's bride. Why had he awakened with this old nightmare of darkness? Although he could feel the foreboding darkness subtly encroaching on the atmosphere of expectation in his home, surely God was on his side and would bless him with a firstborn son. The neighbors, local musicians, and dancers waited outside the door for the announcement. The midwife stepped from behind the drawn curtain with beads of perspiration framing her round face and a darkened countenance. She handed the baby, wrapped in swaddling bands of cloth, to Aiah and said, "I am so sorry for you, Aiah. It's a girl. She's healthy and beautiful, grant you, but nevertheless, she's a girl. Your woes will be many and your rejoicings few with this little one."

Sadness engulfed Aiah and tears filled his eyes as he gazed into the strikingly beautiful eyes of his baby girl. He could feel his footing begin to slip. He could smell the stench and feel the muck and mire of the darkened well of his nightmares. The old familiar melody of "Woe is me!" filled his spirit. He returned the child to the midwife, opened the door, and stepped onto the threshold of his home. The words were like a knot of twisted twine in his throat. His eyes were now brimming with tears that were overflowing down his heartsick countenance. In stunned disbelief, he heard the words come from his mouth as though someone else was speaking them: "It's a girl." He fell to the ground in remorse and shame. Sorrowfully, the neighbors, musicians, and dancers walked away in silence. Once again, the much desired and obvious blessing of God had passed by the door of Aiah.

What good could a baby daughter be?[2] Girls only brought expense to the household. They lacked both intelligence and the ability to take care of you in old age. Everyone knew that! What was the God of heaven thinking when he brought this little girl into his already miserable life?! His wife was beautiful, but she had been barren for so long. With his luck, she might never bear a child again. He would likely never have a son. Woeful lamentations began to fill his mind as frustration and grief filled his groans. What was this daughter to him? Would sad lyrics in minor keys be his forever? What value could she possibly hold? She could do nothing to raise his status or bring encouragement to his days. She was a vanishing zero to him, merely an annoying pebble in the pathway of life.

Days and weeks passed by. Aiah's legs were as heavy as fallen tree trunks. His head hung low while he went about his daily business. His neighbors looked at him with an understanding glance. What name should he give to this insignificant girl? It had been nearly six weeks now; he must come up with a name for her soon. A name came to him out of the depths of the well of his own disappointment. "Rizpah—pavement"[3]—would be her name. An insignificant piece of pavement on the journey of life—that's all she would ever be to him. Her name also meant "hot stone or fiery coal," but "pavement" is all she would ever be to the household of Aiah. She was unwanted and sure to be worthless to him, nothing more than something to walk on.

Here lay this precious gift, a baby girl sent from heaven above for all to adore. All one needed to do was look at her and he or she could see the gift of God shining through her beautiful eyes—little Rizpah, sent from God in heaven to earth below to be a bright and shining light to a generation. Her sightless father could only see the pavement in her, but her heavenly Father destined her to be the hot coal on the fiery tip of a marksman's arrow. This fiery tip would one day proclaim the message of what it means to be a person of destiny with undefeatable faith. She would hit her mark of destiny accurately regardless of others' perspectives. Seen as pavement by mankind but as a firebrand by God above, insignificant to her father but destined to be a rescuer of a generation, this little girl would find her comfort and love not in her earthly father's arms, but in the solace of her heavenly Father on a Rock of refuge and transformation. Her ancestry screeched to her a life of dismay, but her destiny sang a song of deliverance within her hearing. History's claim and destiny's call were two separate voices, one saturated with the perspective of man and the other the perspective of Almighty God.

If you have ever been told that you were insignificant or treated as if you were nothing more than pavement for others to walk on, you can identify with Rizpah's plight. If you have questioned your personal value or been judged based solely on your gender, if you have been plagued by self-doubt about your purpose and worth, you can likely feel the cloud that nearly engulfed Rizpah. Women in 900 B.C.[4] were worth nothing more than a farming implement in their generation; this status was Rizpah's plight. Sadly, although women in the twenty-first century in Europe and North America are purported to be equal in status to their male counterparts, this is often no more than politically correct jargon and holds little truth in the traffic of daily life.

In addressing the issue of the devaluation of women, there is no overt intention to presuppose that men have less value than women. Sadly, women in this generation who are devoid of God's grace and wisdom have forced themselves upon society in such a way that the men of today have become the women of yesterday. Many have lost their way and relinquished their role as leaders and thinkers in the church and society. They are no longer husbands that provide and fathers that influence. Far too many have become ineffective and impotent in their leadership in society, the church, and the home. Their genuine leadership is missed and longed for by women and children. Women everywhere are looking for and desiring for men to step up and offer their marked leadership in all facets of daily life. Men do not have to wait for the invitation to do so; it is their God-given mandate.

However, it must be said that a return to godly leadership is not a return to negative male dominance. It is not a return to the devaluing of women. Little girls everywhere are more than "pavement"; they are "fiery coals" destined to hit a mark (just as every little boy is as well). The future is in the hands of every child, male or female. The recognition of personal value and reaching our destinies is a humanity issue, not a gender issue.

Personal worth is not found in gender, nor is it found in earthly accomplishments, or in salvation for that matter. Destiny is found in God's will and purpose, but personal worth is found in the reality of your simple, yet profound creation. You have worth simply because God created you. That truth is separate from the reality of the wonders of salvation. Regardless of others' perspectives, your perspective, or your accomplishments or failures, you have value. You have worth because of Who created you, not because of who gave birth to you or because of your gender. You do not have worth because of who is proud of you or who is ashamed of you; you have worth because the God of heaven took the time to intricately design you.

I have a beautiful gold chain necklace that was a gift from my husband many years ago. Over the years, due to many miles and not knowing how to properly store and care for the necklace during travel, it became bent in several places. Its beauty was marred to the point that it lost its original luster and is best appreciated in a box of memories in the drawer. Graciously, my husband gave me another beautiful gold chain to replace the damaged one. I am extremely careful with this necklace, and its unmarred beauty has lasted for many years now. Both necklaces were cherished, but both were not well cared for. Which necklace would you say has the greater value?

If melted down into two small golden pools, both necklaces would be of equal value to their creator. To the human eye, the chain without the marks of poor care would have more value, but to the designer of the chains both would be equal.

Prior to your birth and the knowledge of your gender, race, family social status, personal intelligence quotient, personality type, or spiritual gifts, you were simply a child—a child like none other and yet equal to all. A child is a child within the womb, the waiting room of God. One is not more valuable than another. One is not less valuable than another. Each is created equal in the sight of God. Regardless of the scarring or the blessings that may come into the future of every child, each one has worth simply because God cared enough to create him or her.

In Psalm 139:13–16, David proclaims:

Oh yes, you shaped me first inside, then out; you formed me in my mother's womb. I thank you, High God—you're breathtaking! Body and soul, I am marvelously made! I worship in adoration— what a creation! You know me inside and out, you know every bone in my body; You know exactly how I was made, bit by bit, how I was sculpted from nothing into something. Like an open book, you watched me grow from conception to birth; all the stages of my life were spread out before you, the days of my life all prepared before I'd even lived one day. *(The Message)*

David's statement accurately proclaims wonder at the creation of our humanity. Our humanness is a wonder in every facet, and that creation has nothing to do with any influence apart from the Creator Himself. How others influence you or attempt to shape you and what you make of yourself by the grace given to you may affect how you measure your value, but they are not the basis for your personal worth.

Rizpah's father could have seen her through his warped perspective for all the years of his life, and she could have let his perspective shape and restrict her vision, hope, and faith. They both could have estimated her value at the level of pavement. However, their limited perspective would not change God's perspective of her worth. If she were ever going to come out of a "pavement" mentality to a "fiery coal" mentality, she would need to align her perspective with God's, not her father's.

Everyone experiences adversity and most experience some form of prejudice in life. These experiences can break down a healthy perspective on personal worth. We all have breaking points within the confines of our own identity. For example:

+ **Childhood disappointments:** Everything from getting a secondhand tricycle for Christmas to being abused can mark a child's self-perspective.

+ **Imagined abuses:** *They think I'm dumb. They don't like me because I'm not pretty enough or rich enough.* Of course, the questions that beg to be asked in this situation are: What defines smartness? Who defines what pretty is? How rich is rich and what does *rich* mean?

+ **Personal unbroken bondages:** Addictions like drinking, drugs, smoking, masturbation, bulimia, pornography, and many more can affect a person's confidence and perspective on his or her personal worth.

+ **Experienced mental and verbal abuse:** Constant berating in the home and a negative atmosphere can lead to an emotional alignment with the abuser rather than God's positive perspective.

+ **Sexual or physical abuse:** These types of abuse leave a person feeling unworthy and wary of pure love. It leaves him or her with emotions of self-condemnation, anger, hatred and confusion about a truly loving God.

+ **Social status extremes:** Transitioning from riches to poverty or from poverty to riches, growing up with one standard and changing that standard of living in adulthood, can create an identity crisis. Comparisons within the given social circles can create emotions of isolation in an unfamiliar territory.

✦ **Marriage disappointments:** Something in almost every little girl believes in Prince Charming, whether she's ever read Cinderella's story or not. When a young married woman discovers that her prince is not perfect and has "feet of clay," she can become very confused and wonder about her own worth in regard to why God would have allowed her to be married to someone so imperfect. The same could be said for a young husband as he discovers the imperfections of his new bride.

These issues and many more can be breaking points in a person's self-worth. As trials come into every person's life, each must decide how he or she is going to respond. Each person must also decide what to believe when the voice within or the voice of the past begins to tear away at God's perspective of his or her personal worth. Will you succumb to the mired walls of Aiah's terrorizing well? Will you become cracked and worn pavement upon which to walk, like Rizpah's father prophesied in her given name, or will you rise to the status of a firebrand in the hand of a mighty God and make a difference in your world?

So many choices are left in our hands. Some choices evade us, and some remain in our hands until we do something with them. Sadly, ignored choices burden the back of the bearer until they are responded to. Sometimes people think that by not responding to a choice, the issue will just go away. It never does. It simply remains, piling one on top of another, until the person becomes so burdened down that there is nothing to do but respond. Not making a decision is making a decision. Delayed responses are still responses.

If you have been pavement long enough and are weary of letting the choices of your life pile up on you, get up, address the issues, and make a difference in your world. Lay aside what others think you can or cannot do; do what the Lord has told you to do, and let the other voices mutter to themselves in their own wells. Most people who sit in judgment of others are not busying themselves living the lives that God has called them to live. Don't let the "judges" of this world hold you back from living.

A science experiment was done several years ago in a college classroom.[5] The students were given several white mice to run through a maze within a certain time limit. The students were told that the mice had been previously tested and that the first group of white mice was slower than the second. In actuality, the mice had all tested out equally. However, when the students tested them, the mice ran according to the students' belief about them, not according to how they had been previously tested.

This test of the power of belief was then taken into an elementary classroom. The unknowing student teacher was told that certain students were slow learners and that the rest of the class was not. Once again, in actuality the students had been tested previously and had proven to be of equal intelligence. However, under the student teacher's tutelage, the supposed slow learners performed according to what the student teacher believed about them.

What's the lesson here? Others' opinions are not always accurate. Selah; stop and ponder that truth. Others' perspectives, their belief about you or their faith in you, are not always birthed in God's perspective of you. Others are often somewhat blind to the truth of all that you were created to be, and you may be as well. If you buy into anyone's perspective other than God's, you run the risk of purchasing a very limited perspective and coming up short in accurately perceiving your destiny and walking it out in faith.

If you are going to effectively step from the introspective contemplation of your personal worth to destiny and undefeatable faith, you must align your perspective of yourself with God's perspective. When it comes to your personal worth, it does not matter how poorly you have been cared for or what lonesome box someone has placed you in because of life's poor stewardship. Your Creator has a destiny for you to fulfill, and it will only be fulfilled as you grasp hold of the fact that you have worth simply because of Whose you are not who you are.

Let go of the past and reach for the future. Let go of others' perspectives and seek God's. Sometimes people don't let go of the past or its ill-informed and prejudicial pronouncements because they fear the unfamiliar. Even though the past holds them back and pulls them down, they so fear the unfamiliar that they choose to not let go, fearing that they can't. Others have a heritage that is so bright, so positive, and so perfect that they are afraid to let go of it and discover what uniqueness may lie in the pathway that the Lord has for them. They spend their entire life trying to fit into their parents' or grandparents' mold. That too is short-circuiting God's best, as well as His personal revelation of who they are in their own uniqueness. The past and those in it are not always negative. Even the positive and godly can distort your view of who you really are in Him if you never take the time to seek Him personally about it.

God's desire is for all people to step into their unique destiny, having confidence in the knowledge of who they are in Him. If you have a wonderful lineage, respect and honor it, but don't bow down to it. The best way to honor a godly lineage is to discover how God would have you add to it with your own uniqueness. If your lineage is likened to Rizpah's fragile beginnings, one not worthy of your pursuit, then let go of it. It only has hold of you as much as you have hold of it. Let it go. Forgive. Release. Take hold of God's hand and God's perspective. He designed you with joy, not with woeful intentions. He has a great plan ahead. Oh, it's not a plan without challenges, but then, what kind of plan would that be? Reach for the future with courage; there really is a designated plan for you.

Your parentage or your personal journey to this point may shout one perspective to you. It may say that you are no more than pavement and never will be, or it may say that you truly are a firebrand that has been dedicated to the Lord from the time you were in your mother's womb. The past and its varied voices may be history's claim on you, but there is a God in heaven who has a destiny for you that is bigger than your past and bigger than your parents' and grandparents' past. It is your future for better or for worse, filled with mountain peaks and fruit-bearing valleys. Destiny's call to you, not unlike Rizpah's, is that you are to be a fiery coal, a firebrand ready to be placed on the tip of the Master's arrow to hit the target and make your mark on the pages of history. You are called to be a person of undefeatable faith.

My Image in Him

GENESIS 1:26-27: *"Then God said, 'Let Us make man in Our image, according to Our likeness; let them have dominion over the fish of the sea, over the birds of the air, and over the cattle, over all the earth and over every creeping thing that creeps on the earth.' So God created man in His own image; in the image of God He created him; male and female He created them."*

PSALM 139:1-5: *"O LORD, You have searched me and known me. You know my sitting down and my rising up; You understand my thought afar off. You comprehend my path and my lying down, and are acquainted with all my ways. For there is not a word on my tongue, but behold, O LORD, You know it altogether. You have hedged me behind and before, and laid You hand upon me."*

PSALM 139:13-16: *"For You formed my inward parts; You covered me in my mother's womb. I will praise You, for I am fearfully and wonderfully made; Marvelous are Your works, and that my soul knows very well. My frame was not hidden from You, when I was made in secret, And skillfully wrought in the lowest parts of the earth. Your eyes saw my substance, being yet unformed. And Your book they all were written, the days fashioned for me, when as yet there were none of them."*

EPHESIANS 1:17-23: *"I pray for you constantly, asking God, the glorious Father of our Lord Jesus Christ, to give you wisdom to see clearly and really understand who Christ is and all that He has done for you. I pray that your hearts will be flooded with light so that you can see something of the future He has called you to share. I want you to realize that God has been made rich because we who are Christ's have been given to Him! I pray that you will begin to understand how incredibly great His power is to help those who believe Him. It is that same mighty power that raised Christ from the dead and seated Him in the place of honor at God's right hand in* *heaven, far, far above any other king or ruler or dictator or leader. Yes, His honor is far more glorious than that of anyone else either in this world or in the world to come. And God has put all things under His feet and made Him the supreme Head of the church—which is His Body, filled with Himself, the Author and Give of everything everywhere." (TLB)*

1 THESSALONIANS 1:4: *"We know, brothers, that God not only loves you but has selected you for a special purpose." (Phillips)*

EPHESIANS 2:10, 22: *"For we are His workmanship, created in Christ Jesus for good works, which God prepared beforehand that we should walk in them…in whom you also are being built together for a dwelling place of God in the Spirit."*

ISAIAH 49:16: *"See, I have inscribed you on the palms of My hands; Your walls are continually before Me."*

N O T E S

1   Rizpah's father's name means "falcon, vulture, hawk." This may indicate that he was a weak man who benefited from others' hard work and complained (or "screeched" his complaints like a hawk) continually. If his name was indicative of his character, he probably was not a pleasant father under which to grow up. Rizpah was likely not considered valuable and did not grow up in a faith-filled atmosphere. See *Strong's Concordance, Bible Works*, #0345; *Hitchcock Bible Names, E-Sword*; and *Webster E-Sword*.

2   "Daughters were not so highly prized as sons, not being usually mentioned by name. A father might sometimes sell his daughter as bondwoman (Ex. 21:7); though not to a foreigner (Ex. 21:8); daughters might sometimes inherit as did sons, but could not take the inheritance outside of the tribe (Nu. 36:1-12)." *International Standard Bible Encyclopedia; Bible Works;* #15620; 2540.02

3   The meaning of Rizpah's name: The name "pavement" could be indicative of the fact that in her culture and generation she had little value as a woman and as a daughter. She was easily "walked on" in her culture and generation. The name "coal; hot stone" may be interpreted as meaning that she was destined by God to make a firebrand mark on her generation. Name meanings derived from *Easton Dictionary, Bible Works; Strong's Concordance, Bible Works;* #7532; *International Standard Bible Encyclopedia; E-Sword.*

4   Kevin Conner and Ken Malmin, *Old Testament Survey*, rev. (Portland, OR: City Bible Publishing, Formerly Bible Temple Publishing, 1975), II Samuel.

5   This story is paraphrased from Glenda Malmin, *The Hidden Power of a Surrendered Life* (Portland, OR: City Bible Publishing, 2002), 27.

Trust in the Master's Plan

Today's Dilemma, Tomorrow's Hope

And Saul had a concubine, whose name was Rizpah — 2 Samuel 3:7

From the time Rizpah was three years old, Aiah demanded that she beg at the nearby street corner. If she did not bring in an ample supply of shekels, little Rizpah had to go one block further away the next day and beg for more. If that didn't work, she would have to go three blocks from home the next day. No matter how frightening a new neighborhood or corner was for her, she had to go. Some days her father would hide behind a corner building and watch after her, and some days he would not. He would roughly drag her by the nape of her neck and leave her on the corner with a bit of bread and a bag for shekels that was nearly as big as she was.

He cared little that she stood on the corner so many days with unending tears staining her dirty little dress while dogs that belonged only to the streets came and licked at her scabbed knees. He cared little that older children glared at her and sometimes spit on her and that passing men touched her matted hair and invited her in to dark places and that women raised their eyebrows at her. On her tear-filled days, he spitefully said to her, "Tears bring in more money from one your size anyway; cry as much as you want."

Tears didn't move Aiah, nor did they seem to annoy him. However if she whined, like he constantly did, he threatened to cut off one of her legs to the knee so that passersby would have pity on her and give her more. Fearing that he would indeed follow through on his threat, tiny Rizpah always worked hard to beg from those dressed in the finest of apparel, as well as any others who might pass by her corner. By the time she was five years old, she hardly ever cried. She had come to realize that on most days her bright smile and flashing brown eyes could earn more shekels than a saddened countenance or dripping tears. By the time she was seven she had become very skilled at reading dress styles and body language and could discern who would have the most to give and who might be the most willing to give it.

From a very young age, five or six she thought, Rizpah had disciplined and trained herself to be logical about most events in her life. Being logical and unemotional had become such a lifestyle that she could barely remember when this discipline really became part of her. Due to her father's brutish and demanding ways, and her mother dying in childbirth when she was only two years old, Rizpah had developed this skill earlier than most, she reckoned. She heard through the neighborhood grapevine that both of her grandmothers had died at what many considered premature ages. Why was it that women died so easily and men lived so woefully? It had been a long time since tears had come to her eyes; in fact she could not remember the last time she could feel the sting of tears filling her eyes and running down her cheeks. Her father only looked out for his own good, always bemoaning his woes, never caring for hers. He constantly reminded her of what a burden she was to him and how worthless she was. He provided little and demanded much. She did more work for her father than any girl her age; even the neighbor next door said so. Surely that was some kind of proof—that neighbor seemed to know everything about everyone on the block.

The older Rizpah got, the more skilled she became at begging. Though her father always wanted her to bring home money, her favorite thing to receive was soap that would wash both her body and her hair.

When Aiah wasn't watching, she would almost always ask for soap, especially the kind that made her beautiful, thick raven-black hair soft to the touch. One Tuesday a month, on the corner three blocks from home, some very kind maidens would give her leftover crushed coal on small paint pallets so that she could beautify her eyes. On a really good day, when she ventured closer to the marketplace four blocks away, some equally generous ladies would give her an occasional scrap of fabric or a scarf. That was her special delight. When that happened, she immediately braided it into her hair, or into a belt for her coverlet. It was never much, but it always made an appealing colorful accessory according to her estimation. If she got more than enough material, she would make a new head covering for her father in hopes that he would compliment her work—ever listening for the compliments, but never receiving them.

On one of Rizpah's begging excursions near the marketplace, an old woman with a tender countenance called to her. She was sitting near the end of market-row with a basket of long fabric swatches, busily embroidering them with fine threads of purple, red, and gold. It was lunchtime and Rizpah was tired and hungry, so she responded to her by sitting next to her basket of unfinished cloths. The old woman, noticing her small bit of bread, offered her some olives and a bit of dipping oil for her bread and a delicious pomegranate as well. She remembered that first lunch as if it were yesterday. She could, in fact, still taste the succulence of the pomegranate if she really gave her thoughts to it for very long.

The old woman's name was Phoebe.[1] Rizpah thought that was quite a fitting name for her; it meant "pure, radiant as the moon." Phoebe, though old and wrinkled to the natural eye, was certainly pure of heart and radiant in countenance. She had a giggle that was unmatched by anyone Rizpah knew. Just by the sparkle in her eye and the turn of her head, which always indicated that a delightful giggle was soon approaching, she could make Rizpah laugh. Phoebe became her constant lunch companion and taught her lessons about Jehovah as they talked.

They did this almost daily for three years. Rizpah learned that in spite of her circumstances, there was a God in heaven who knew her and cared about her deeply. She learned that He listened to her prayers and saw her every deed, as well as the deeds of others, including her father. She learned that He also was very aware of every circumstance that surrounded her and that He rewarded those that trusted in Him. Phoebe also told her that Jehovah had a great plan for her life and that even though her father could only see the "pavement," Jehovah had destined for her to be a hot fiery coal on the tip of an arrow that would one day make a mark on her generation. Phoebe told her that she was special to Him and that He loved her with an everlasting love.

These were amazing thoughts to Rizpah. She had never experienced caring love or unselfish provision before. Old Phoebe spoon-fed these heart-penetrating truths to Rizpah day-by-day for three years; she massaged them into her very soul until Rizpah fully embraced them. Surely there must be a God in heaven that saw and cared. Although Rizpah's daily life circumstances provided no evidence for any of these assertions, she did believe that she had a purpose and that she was not forever destined to just be pavement for others to walk and spit on. She would choose to dream the dream of God, not the nightmares and hopeless predictions of her father.

Her heart rejoiced in the possibility that she could be a fiery tip on an arrow in the hand of a mighty God, destined to hit a target and make her mark. It had to be true. All Hebrews believed in destiny. Even her father and grandfather believed in destiny—though it was a negative one. She would choose to believe in a positive destiny, one orchestrated and designed by a mighty God who cared. Tenderhearted old Phoebe was the only person who had ever shown kindness toward Rizpah, and Phoebe believed in the destiny of God, so why shouldn't she? Phoebe's life had not been easy either, and yet she believed.

Phoebe mentored Rizpah in the truth that a person has choice. There was destiny, but there was also choice. She taught Rizpah that faith was more about choosing and trusting than about the visible circumstances that surrounded you—that you could, in fact, have faith that was undefeatable if you chose to trust Jehovah. You could either choose to believe the worst and watch it come, or you could choose to believe Jehovah God and watch for the fulfillment of His will to be worked out in His mysterious way.

Choosing and *trusting* were like synonyms to the aged Phoebe, and somehow those words had adhered to Rizpah's soul and became more to her than words. She wasn't sure exactly why. They just had. *To choose is to trust and to trust is to choose.* This was the lesson of the aged mentor. These were more than words; they were a formula by which Rizpah would live.

Apart from the joy of her lunches with Phoebe, the discipline of choosing her thought patterns and responses was the only way Rizpah could sustain her sanity in her childhood and young womanhood. Now it was the only way to sustain it in the reality of her adult world as well. Granted, she was only fourteen years of age, but in her world a fourteen-year-old was an adult, especially for a young woman. No longer could she simply stand on a street corner and beg without being solicited inappropriately. It became more wearing on her emotions every day, especially since her noontime encouragement from Phoebe was no longer a part of her day. It had been several months since she had seen the tenderhearted old woman, and she worried about her.

But for today, regardless of her father's complaints, threats, or disarmingly unusual quietness, there would be no logic, no begging, and no early morning chores. (Maybe her father's quietness was his expression of regret for the choices he made, likely not.) Nevertheless, Rizpah's newfound hormones raged, and her mood swings led her to these amaranthine emotional contemplations of earlier years. They drove her back into the wilderness of her soul and memories of the genuine cruelty of her father, but also to the joys of her conversations with aged Phoebe and the places of her girlhood hopes and dreams.

She could still remember the dreams she had of marrying Joshua, the boy who lived three blocks from her home. She could still see him coming by her corner to flirt with her. He was named after the great leader Joshua, Moses' successor. Surely he was destined to be a great leader too! She had longed for him to beseech his father that he might make a betrothal offer to Aiah. If only he would her world would surely change from a never-ending atmosphere of misery and hardship to a new life in which her destiny could be reached, just like Phoebe had predicted.

This had been her prayer—her hope. She longed to make a difference in her world. She had a faith tucked away in her heart that would not leave her, even in the midst of the oppressive stench of her father's lifestyle. This faith had not come easily to Rizpah, as it did to others who grew up with loving parents and no need to beg on the streets. She worked hard at fighting off the negative ancestral recording within her own mind. Phoebe's words and the words of Jehovah were her constant companions. Yet still, how easy it was to think negative thoughts; after all, the entire atmosphere of her home and life was woefully negative. She actually couldn't remember ever hearing a positive word come from her father or grandfather. But somehow she could see sunshine on cloudy days and feel a loving embrace from heaven above even on a cold and rainy day. Most days she could turn her father's woeful whining into a playful melody within her ears, and daily she chose for his constant demands to become her delightful opportunities to serve. The mentoring words of dear old Phoebe rang in her ears even when her heart wanted to give in to a life of woe as well.

Rizpah recognized that, due to her circumstances, she had a strength that other girls did not seem to have, but she still hoped within the quietness of her heart to one day be released from being a second-rate daughter to being the beautiful wife of one who would love and adore her. This was her hope, this was her dream—to be a virtuous wife and happy mother.

But then it happened. Her father, Aiah, came to her with the news. She would no longer need to go to the marketplace to beg. There would be no more downward glances or inappropriate solicitations; he had something "better" for her. But the look on his countenance conveyed that it was something better for *him*, not for her. Had her faith in Jehovah led her to a bogus pretension? Had her hopes and dreams falsely led her to imagine a life of joy in the future? How had she forgotten her father's control over her, his disdain for her, and his self-focused ambition? It was bad enough that she was a daughter in a son's world, but now her father had offered her as a concubine—not a wife, but a concubine. She would be doomed to this secondary fate forever. Granted, Aiah said that he had offered her to King Saul, which would be considered a step up to many, but she had no desire to be a concubine, a "second wife." She wanted to be a wife, a first wife, even if it was to the poorest of the poor.

For a mere pittance of recompense, her father had offered her up on the throne of greed and self-gratification.[2] To be considered a father-in-law of King Saul would only inflate Aiah's own ego and aggrandize his status within the neighborhood.[3] There was no thought whatsoever for Rizpah's welfare in this decision; it was merely a business deal for Aiah. There was no regard for her—there never had been and there never would be.

Aiah had always been a whining swindler, and this was the ultimate swindle. He had given her false hope by speaking with Joshua's father just two weeks prior. How could he do this? She had never done him any harm. It was not her fault that she was a daughter and not a son. How fair could this be? How much could this concubinage business transaction really have added to his status or his bank account?

It was bad enough to be considered second in importance in her father's home because of her gender, but now she would also be considered secondary in the home of the man who would father her children. To be a concubine, a second wife, was the least of her dreams. Indeed, she had hoped to be free from her father and the constant barrage of berating assaults. She had prayed to Jehovah for deliverance and believed that He had heard her prayer when Joshua's father made such a handsome betrothal proposal to Aiah two weeks ago. Little did she know King Saul had seen her in the marketplace the following week, and his eye had landed on her. He had made his own offer to her father the very next day—not to be a wife, but rather a concubine.

When would her life change? Of what value was she? Would she always be second-class? Phoebe had told her that class had nothing to do with value, but second is second. Everyone knew that. Was Jehovah the great equalizer? Was there really a God in heaven after all? She had struggled to stay positive in heart and to believe that the Almighty heard her prayers. Did He see her? Did He see any value in her? Would her status ever change? Would she forever remain second in the eyes of God and man?

Although Rizpah's tears had ceased to flow long ago, hopes had not ceased to build within her heart and her spirit. This was especially true since kind old Phoebe had come into her life and Jehovah had become so real to her. Truth be known, she had invited Jehovah to be a part of her reality, part of her very being, the second week after she met Phoebe. It was as though they had both given her permission to dream for the first time in her life. Had dear sweet Phoebe been an angel in disguise? She was so wise, so kind, and so wealthy in spirit and in heart. Rizpah loved to be in her presence, sitting and listening, being mentored by her words, even by the very gestures of her expressive hands. How many times had they knelt to pray together by that basket of fabric pieces? How often had they relished in the bright future ahead for Rizpah? What hope, what vision, had been planted in Rizpah's heart? Though her days with her father had dragged on, the weeks and months being mentored at Phoebe's knee had vanished all too quickly.

Where was the aged Phoebe now? How Rizpah longed to hear her words of wisdom once again. She had not been at the corner with her old familiar basket for at least six months now. *"Phoebe, Phoebe, where are you?"* All she could hear ricocheting off the walls of her mind was, *"Concubine, concubine, second wife, second one, worthless one!"* She fell into a crumpled, weeping pile near the old cookstove.

"Jehovah, Jehovah, speak to me. Your servant listens!" Somehow, in the midst of the anguish and turmoil of her soul, Rizpah could hear not only Phoebe's echoing words of encouragement, but that strong yet gentle whisper of Jehovah as well. Dear old Phoebe had mentored her wisely in how to call on Jehovah and hear His wise and merciful words. She had often said of late, "Earthly mentors come and go, but Jehovah never leaves or forsakes." [4] Jehovah was the One who would lead and guide her

throughout life regardless of what may come. She believed with a faith that could not be turned away that He could hear the questions of her heart and the pleadings of her soul.

"Please, Jehovah God, hear my petitions today! Answer my questions, I beseech You earnestly! Is second really second? What value and what hope could I possibly have now? A concubine...I have been slotted to be a "second" forever! Jehovah, I beseech You earnestly, with sincerity in my heart, how on this earth and in this generation will I ever make a difference being a lowly concubine?"

How devastating it must have been for Rizpah, one who so longed to find acceptance and true love, to now become a concubine. Although concubinage at this time in history was not as horrible for some as it might be presumed, it was still somewhat tenuous. As a concubine, Rizpah would have been considered as a second wife to King Saul. She would have more privileges than other slaves, but not the same privileges that a wife would have. She would be conjugally united to the king, but in a relationship that was considered inferior to that of a wife, having no authority or privileges in the household.[5]

Can you hear Rizpah's cry? Can you identify with her seemingly hopeless quandary? Perhaps you cannot identify with her specific circumstances—they are likely different than yours. Yet the heart-issues and truths of her story ring true to the heart of most people today. She wanted to be loved for who she was, not for what she could do or what she could provide. She wasn't born into a perfect family with a flawless financial statement and desirable social standing. Neighbors weren't lined up at their door waiting for a dinner invitation. People in her life put burdens and expectations on her that were unbearable at times. She had family members that she wouldn't have introduced to the neighbor's dog, and yet she still longed for their approval. Her daily atmosphere was negative, not positive. The walls of her home were darkened by years of pain and suffering, not shining with impeccable perfection and joyful family life.

She longed to not only be significant to someone, but to actually *be significant.* She yearned to find fulfillment in something other than a role or what she could provide for another person. She worked hard to be more than a B in an A world. She strove to be chosen, but was forever left behind. Her past had a way of not only haunting her, but of seemingly hunting her down and claiming her present as well as her future.

Rizpah had a faith that was mysteriously undefeatable—even to her. She had a desire to make a difference in her generation, yet her faith was constantly challenged and her hopes stepped on with one heavy foot after the other. Through all that life had dealt her thus far, there remained a determination in her heart and a faith that was supernaturally under-girded by God. This faith was so deep that circumstances, ancestral quicksand, or the demons of hell could not pull it from her. This faith was within her very core; its transforming power was changing her from pavement to a hot fiery coal, fit for the Master's use.

First Corinthians 10:11 says of those who lived in Old Testament times, "Now all these things happened to them as examples, and they were written for our admonition." Rizpah's life and the record of her story is for you. She lived her life not unto herself, but for you—it is for you to read, to feel, and to ponder. She was not unlike you. She needed strength; she needed hope. She needed faith, and she chose it. You also need strength, hope, and faith, and you too can choose it. When you do, that faith becomes undefeatable, just like Rizpah's. When you adhere your will to the will of the Master, your faith becomes impenetrable.

Faith is not based on heritage, personality-type, or pleasant circumstances. Faith is a choice, and yes, it can be undefeatable if you choose for it to be. Granted, it does appear to come more easily to some than to others due to personality-type or life circumstances. For example, some believe that it's easy for Americans to have faith for big things because they live in a big nation and even easier for Texans because they live in a big state in a big nation. Some believe that it's easier for sanguine personality-types to have faith than for melancholy personality-types because sanguine-types are naturally more joyful. Some believe that it's easier for the wealthy to have faith because they have more to work with than those who are poor.

If all of this were true, why is it that so many Americans are on antidepressants, country music is laden with sad lyrics, sanguine-types have emotional lows that match their emotional highs, and the wealthy are so often known for pinching every penny that crosses their desktops? Faith is not about circumstances; it's about faith. Circumstances may contribute to an individual's walk of faith, but they do not create faith.

Hebrews 11:1 says, "Now faith is the substance of things hoped for, the evidence of things not seen." It goes on in verse 6, "But without faith it is impossible to please Him, for he who comes to God must believe that He is, and He is a rewarder of those who diligently seek Him."

Rizpah had to have faith for blessing and purpose in her life that went beyond what she could see and the preconceived ideas and identity definitions that she could give to her own life. Why? Because she had a limited perspective on her life. We all do. Rizpah had to have faith in the heavenly Rewarder in order to walk and not stumble through the journey of life with any semblance of sanity and hope. Again, we all do. She had to choose not only to believe, but also to trust. As you could guess, we all do. The combination of belief and trust is a wonderful recipe for faith, for today's dilemma is often tomorrow's hope. The price? Trust in the Master and His plan.

Each of us faces dilemmas, whether we are rich or poor, sick or healthy, sanguine or melancholy. Each of us must choose faith; we must look for the hope in tomorrow's sunrise. That's what trust in the Master is all about: *To choose is to trust and to trust is to choose.* Faith is about choosing to trust the Lord Jesus Christ in the circumstances of your daily life. You alone cannot change your circumstances, but you can trust the One who can change them or bring you through them. You have a limited perspective on your life, but God doesn't. You have lived on this earth only as long as the actual years you have lived, but God has been in existence for eternity and saw and numbered your days even before you were in your mother's womb.[6]

You will never learn faith in comfortable surroundings. God gives us His promises in a quiet hour, seals our covenants with great and gracious words, and then steps back, waiting to see how much we believe. He then allows the Tempter to come, and the ensuing test seems to contradict all that He has spoken. This is when faith wins its crown. This is the time to look up through the storm, and…declare, "I have faith in God that it will happen just as he told me" (Acts 27:25).[7]

Faith is not a lone target with a specific circumstance that provides the marking place for the arrow; the journey of your life provides it. There is not just one targeted circumstance in life that you are aiming for; it's a targeted life that walks and moves from one circumstance to another that counts. Too often people are looking for one dramatic situation in which to let their faith shine, but undefeatable faith is more than that. It's not one isolated incident at the end of life; it's a series of circumstances along the way. It's the faith to believe that God is leading your life carefully and thoughtfully regardless of the surrounding circumstances. It's the faith to keep on going and not give up in the face of insurmountable odds. It's when you truly align your faith with the Master's, surrendering completely to Him, that it becomes impenetrable and absolutely undefeatable.

Reasons Why I Have Value

GENESIS 1:26: *I am created in the image of God. "Then God said, 'Let Us make man in Our image, according to Our likeness.'"*

ISAIAH 40:11: *God cares about me and will lead me carefully through life. "Like a shepherd, he will care for his flock, gathering the lambs in his arms, hugging them as he carries them, leading the nursing ewes to good pasture." (The Message)*

ISAIAH 49:1: *God has called me from the time I was in my mother's womb. "The LORD has called Me from the womb; from the matrix of My mother He has made mention of My name."*

ISAIAH 49:15–16: *God carries a picture of me with Him constantly. "I will not forget you. See, I have engraved you on the palms of my hands; your walls are continually before Me."*

PSALM 139:16: *God prepared the journey of my life before I even arrived on earth. "Like an open book, you watched me grow from conception to birth; all the stages of my life were spread out before you, the days of my life all prepared before I'd even lived one day." (The Message)*

1 CORINTHIANS 3:16: *God's Presence dwells in me. "Do you not know that you are the temple of God and that the Spirit of God dwells in you?"*

2 CORINTHIANS 5:17: *I am a new creation in Christ. "Therefore, if anyone is in Christ, he is a new creation; old things have passed away; behold, all things have become new."*

EPHESIANS 1:4: *I am chosen. "He chose us in Him before the foundation of the world, that we should be holy and without blame before Him in love."*

EPHESIANS 1:5: *I am God's child. "…having predestined us to adoption as sons by Jesus Christ to Himself, according to the good pleasure of His will."*

EPHESIANS 1:6: *God accepts me right now. "…to the praise of the glory of His grace, by which He made us accepted in the Beloved."*

EPHESIANS 2:10: *I am God's work of art. "For we are His workmanship, created in Christ Jesus for good works, which God prepared beforehand that we should walk in them."*

1 JOHN 2:12: *God cares so much about me that He has forgiven me. "I write to you, little children, because your sins are forgiven you for His name's sake."*

I have value because God, the Creator of the universe, created me, cares for me, and paid a price for me. Selah.

NOTES

1   Though "Phoebe" will become a significant character in my story of Rizpah, the reader should know that she is fictional. It is not difficult to suppose that such an amazing mentor was a likely possibility in a story such as this, however the Bible account never speaks of such a person.

2   "The state of concubinage is assumed and provided for by the law of Moses. A concubine would generally be either (1) a Hebrew girl bought of her father; (2) a Gentile captive taken in war; (3) a foreign slave bought; or (4) a Canaanitish woman, bond or free. The rights of the first two were protected by the law, Ex. 21:7; Deut. 21:10-14; but the third was unrecognized and the fourth prohibited. Free Hebrew women also might become concubine." William Smith, L.L.D., rev. and ed. by F. N. and M. A. Peloubet, *A Dictionary of the Bible* (Nashville, TN: Thomas Nelson, 1813–1893), 122.

3   "In Judg. 19 the possessor of a concubine was called her 'husband,' her father is called the 'father-in-law,' and he the 'son-in-law,' showing how nearly the concubine approached to the wife." Merrill F. Unger, *Unger's Bible dictionary* (Chicago: Moody Press, 1966), 217.

4   "Let your conduct be without covetousness; be content with such things as you have. For He Himself has said, 'I will never leave you nor forsake you.'" (Hebrews 13:5)

5   "Concubine, in the Bible denotes a female conjugally united to a man, but in a relation inferior to that of a wife. Among the early Jews, from various causes, the difference between a wife and a concubine was less marked than it would be amongst us. The concubine was a wife of secondary rank. There are various laws recorded providing for their protection Ex 21:7 De 21:10-14 and setting limits to the relation they sustained to the household to which they belonged Ge 21:14 25:6. they had no authority in the family, nor could they share in the household government." *Easton Dictionary; Bible Works*, #00875

6   "Then the word of the LORD came to me, saying: 'Before I formed you in the womb I knew you; Before you were born I sanctified you; I ordained you a prophet to the nations.'" (Jeremiah 1:4–5)

7   L. B. Cowman, ed. James Reimann, *Streams in the Desert: 266 Daily Devotional Readings* (Grand Rapids, MI: Zondervan, 1997), 18.

Dreams Realized, Hopes Narrowed

The Confines of This Earth

...Armoni and Mephibosheth, the two sons of Rizpah the daughter of Aiah, whom she bore to Saul — 2 Samuel 21:8

With strands of hair falling loosely around her face, the haphazardly woven braid hanging down her back began to ravel apart. When sleep would not return to her, Rizpah lit the blackened oil lamp and awakened her sleeping maidens. She then gave each of them specific tasks so that the three of them together might be able to complete the job with haste. She felt the urge to clean her quarters even though the sun had not yet peaked over the horizon, so much to their chagrin she busied both herself and her maidens. Rizpah was great with child and could tell in her body that the day of delivery was upon her. Suddenly her grasp on the broom loosened as she felt her abdomen tighten with pain. Breathing slowly and deeply, she soon felt the cramping wave begin to diminish in its intensity.

Perspiration beads glistened on her forehead as the sunrise began to shine through the open doorway. Her countenance glowed in the morning light, as if to quietly say to the One who created it and to the little one who rested securely beneath her heart, "You are both welcome in this place." As the pangs of early labor subsided, Rizpah took pause and sat on the purple cushion nearby as she drank in the fresh morning air for just a few moments. Now realizing what was happening to their mistress, her maidens scurried around the room completing the early morning assignments given them.

While her maidens continued to sweep and dust every nook and cranny visible to the human eye, Rizpah reached for the laundry awaiting her attention in the oversized straw basket nearby. Breathing deeply while moving her hand slowly across her swollen abdomen, she finished folding the last few swaddling bands in preparation for the babe that was about to be born.

The cloth bands, made of tightly woven lamb's wool, felt soft to her touch. She began to imagine how soft and how dear a new baby would soon feel in her arms and wondered how soft these freshly folded swaddling clothes would feel next to her newborn's skin. She pondered how many immediate adjustments this tiny one would be required to make. A dry world instead of a wet one, light instead of darkness, and an abrupt decline in "room" temperature would all be strange and shocking to one so new to the world. Breathing air for life-sustaining oxygen and experiencing the gravity pull of his or her weight rather than tumbling freely within the womb would be new and unfamiliar sensations as well. Rizpah's thoughts were startled back to reality when a new wave of pain began to increase in her abdomen. Though life "on the outside" might be unfamiliar to the child within her womb, from all indications he or she was apparently determined to make an entrance soon.

The laundry was done, the basins washed, and the floor swept clean—even the plants were dusted. Her two young maidens were exhausted from Rizpah's early morning impetuous demands to get the cleaning done so speedily. Although they were tired, Rizpah's sudden surge of energy still remained with her. She was now ready...or was she?

The noontime sun shone through the doorway— time had passed quickly with all the cleaning and folding of laundry. Feeling another pain coming at a closer interval and lasting longer than the previous one,

Rizpah breathed in deeply and then exhaled over the top of the wave of pain. She then sent one of her young maidens to fetch the midwife. Anxious thoughts filled her mind as she pondered whether this child would be a daughter, which would be considered a burden, or a son, which would be admired. Although she realized that every child was a gift from Jehovah and knew that she would love either gender, she also knew that a second son would give her more clout with King Saul.

Her thoughts went immediately to little Armoni, her firstborn child. She had sent a message to the nursemaid to keep him for the day when she realized that the pangs of labor were upon her. What a beautiful child he was with his dancing brown eyes and curly black hair. His features were as handsome as King Saul's, and although he was only two, he was already big for his age. Everyone who saw him wondered if he would be tall like his father. It was she who had suggested the name Armoni for him, and Saul had been impressed. Armoni means "palatial, grand, to be elevated." [1] Saul readily agreed that name would be fitting for any of his sons; no one in all of history had been named Armoni before. Saul's interest in Rizpah had been sparked afresh with her progressive and bold suggestion, and he agreed gladly to the child's name. He adored Armoni, though it had been five months since he had seen him due to the continuous warring in the land.

Although the birth of another son might impress Saul, it could intimidate Saul's wife, Ahinoam. [2] It could potentially bring about disfavor in her eyes. Rizpah's dreams could be realized and yet her hopes narrowed if she found disfavor in Ahinoam's eyes. Though her sons could have legal rights to the throne of Saul, as a concubine she virtually had no rights apart from whatever benevolence Saul's wife afforded her. What should she hope for, a son or a daughter? A son would bring pleasure to Saul, but a daughter would more easily find favor with Ahinoam since Rizpah already had little Armoni. Even though Ahinoam had four sons and two daughters and should not be easily intimidated, one could never know for sure what went on in a royal mind. Rizpah's emotions, prayers, and desires were colliding within her anxiously.

Old Phoebe would have told her to trust in Jehovah, and she knew this was what she must continue to do. Actually, Rizpah and Jehovah had become quite close since Saul had taken her to be his concubine, and Phoebe had disappeared from their familiar meeting place not long after. Phoebe's voice still rang in her ears from time to time, but Jehovah's still small voice whispered words of faith and confidence to her. She had become quite comfortable in His Presence and depended on His encouragement daily, especially of late. The pressure of giving birth to another heir of Saul was immense; every eye was on her, wondering whether it would be a son or a daughter.

Without realizing it, she could hear herself speaking tersely to her residing young attendant, demanding to know when the midwife was going to arrive. Hearing such an uncharacteristic and unforeseen tone come from her own mouth, Rizpah humbly apologized to the startled young girl. Now feeling another birth pang beginning to move across her middle, she cried out to Jehovah to help her. As she did so, the midwife arrived and everything seemed calm for one brief shining moment as the pain abated. More pillows were placed behind her back to prop her up into an upright position, and the attending maiden was sent to get the water that was kept hot on the coal pit grill. She was also told to send the messenger boy to alert the local musicians and dancers of the imminent birth.

Surprisingly, within minutes Rizpah felt the urge to push the child from within her womb to its earthly station in life. She squeezed the hand of the young maiden by her side and raised herself from the bed to a squatting position. She heard the midwife call to the returning maiden to bring the basin of water and more cloths quickly. No more daydreaming, all of her energies and thoughts were now focused. Rizpah pushed again, and then the midwife told her she must wait for the next wave. She felt as though she would rather burst than wait another minute—more breathing and more patience were the command of the seemingly eternal moment. The beads of perspiration that had crowned her brow earlier now dripped from her forehead. Then came the next surge of pain. With the midwife's firm command to push with everything within her, she cried out to Jehovah with intensity. Then suddenly the strong cry of a healthy baby filled the room—what sweet melody to her ears! Tears of joy filled her eyes. All praise to Jehovah, the delivery of this child with such a thunderous voice had been relatively swift and without complication.

All four women present were now weeping with joy. The midwife wrapped the babe in the prepared swaddling bands and handed him to Rizpah tenderly saying, "Rejoice, daughter of Jehovah, you have a son." Rizpah looked into the eyes of her newborn babe and rejoiced at the goodness of a mighty God, knowing that she must soak in this moment of unadulterated peace and joy, for it was the calm before the unknown, yet ensuing storm. Her very soul was saturated with the peace of God; contentment flooded her being. Rizpah's heart rejoiced and she spoke softly the prayer of her predecessor Hannah: "My heart rejoices in the Lord; in the Lord my horn is lifted high.... There is no one holy like the Lord; there is no one besides you; there is no Rock like our God." [3] Then out of the abundance of her own heart she prayed, "*Oh Lord, my refuge and my fortress, my rock, in whom I trust, I praise You for the protection of Your Presence. Thank You for laying this little child in my arms to love and to cherish. Help me, his mother, always to dwell under the shadow of the Almighty, in the secret place of the Most High.*" [4] In the purity of her rejoicing and her proclamations of trust, Rizpah surrendered afresh to Jehovah as she dedicated her newborn son to Him.

Rizpah then handed her tiny son back to the midwife, knowing that she had sent for the neighborhood musicians and dancers. She must now present this potential heir to the throne to the celebrants and announce the news that he was indeed a son of Saul—then the rejoicing would begin. Rizpah would then nurse him by her side while the music played outside her door, and all would be well with the world.

Saul was away at war, but a courier was sent with the message right away. Rizpah knew that the news of a new son would be an encouragement to him on the field of battle, and this would bring her joy. Though she disdained being a concubine, she did have a love for her king and the father of her sons. In fact, her heart and desire for him surprised even her at times. It went deep into her soul in ways that she could not explain. She would be forever loyal to Saul, for he had shown her tenderness in intimacy and generosity in provision.

She desired to name her new son Mephibosheth, "one who dispels the shame of Baal; to scatter." [5] She prayed that one day he would expose the shame of Baal and scatter the news of the wonders of Jehovah abroad.

When Saul arrived home three weeks later, he joyfully confirmed Rizpah's wish, and the child was named Mephibosheth. Her earnest desire was that her two sons would be honorable in the eyes of the people and that they would be elevated to high positions as they grew in the wisdom of God and man. She desired for them to be righteous and just and to make a difference in their generation. Her constant prayer was that they would not get lost in the ordinariness of life that could engulf those in lower stations. She wanted them to be noteworthy men, blameless in the sight of men and God.

Although these were days of war within the nation, the ensuing months and years of parenting her growing sons were ones of quiet delight in Rizpah's heart. King Saul was focused on battle strategies, while she gave her full attention to her treasures, Armoni and Mephibosheth. She realized that she was merely a concubine of Saul, and her hopes of being first in importance in anything were a distant memory. The turmoil of the warring emotions of personal surrender and significance within her had all but vanished years ago. She now accepted her lot in life and found great joy in mothering Armoni and Mephibosheth.

Although her dreams of being a mother had been realized, she was clearly cognizant of her personal limitations apart from the hope that her sons would one day have a place of prominence in the kingdom. She also found solace and peace in the light of Jehovah—He was her constant source of encouragement. There was in fact an underlying faith within Rizpah that her son's lives would make a difference. Even if significance and prominence were never to be hers, their lives would count.

That faith never left her; it was immovable. She believed deeply that the fulfillment of these hopes and dreams was the will of her loving and faithful Jehovah God.

Rizpah's trust in God was crucial. Although her concubinage had narrowed her hopes, her dreams of motherhood had been realized and had likely raised those hopes again. However, her future would reveal that her hope was not to be found in that which she may have supposed. It would not be found in earthbound places of prominence for her sons or any other temporal provision. It would not be found in a palace or on an earthly throne, but on a Rock instead.

What underlying faith runs deep within you while remaining unseen by many? Have you given up on it, or does it still beat within your heart? Does this faith still have a focus, a hope, a desire that will not leave your thoughts for many days at a time? Has it taken on new definition and possibilities as the circumstances and seasons of life have presented themselves before you? Are your dreams somewhat realized while your hopes have been narrowed by the confines of this earth?

I am a firm believer in blossoming wherever God has planted you. I think Rizpah was too. I believe that people, by our own definitions of God's calling and destiny for our lives, get hemmed into a life of futility and frustration. We do it to ourselves, all the while blaming others. We read a Scripture, hear God whisper to us in our devotional times, or even receive a personal prophetic word from one of God's intuitive servants— only to take that word and add our own definitions to it.

For example, God may have spoken to you about being a pastor, which you may have defined as being a full-time, on-staff elder in a church. That may not be what God meant at all. He may desire to prosper you in the secular workforce and have you "pastor" or be pastoral toward those who do not know Him personally, as well as people in the church.

All believers are called to gently shepherd those that God puts in their care. Rather than pastoring a congregation on Sunday mornings, God may desire to fill you with His Word and enable you to minister effectively to a small group in the church. He may not want to limit your influence to a church staff position. Leading and caring for a small group of people is pastoring. Personally, I have found that people will often tell lay pastors and lay leaders detailed concerns on their hearts that they will *never* tell ordained pastors for fear that they may be ostracized for their questions and concerns.

Granted, you are likely not a concubine, but you too may feel like you are in a tenuous or ineffective position and that your only hope of marked influence is through your children, either natural or spiritual. That may, in fact, be true in the eyes of man, but it is not true in the eyes of God. God's measuring rod for fruitfulness and effectiveness is much different from mankind's. What is important to God is obedience, while what seemingly is important to man is gifting and position. Obedience is the foundation stone of undefeatable faith.

God cares little about your position and how narrow it may appear to you or anyone else. He does care, however, about how you'll use what He gives you and your perspective and attitude. He wants you to enjoy the journey. Joy releases faith and faith releases joy. He cares greatly about your obedience and wants you to enjoy what He has planned for you. You are vital to His plan. He has predestined, preplanned, and preordained your steps. You are on His timeline, not your own (or anyone else's for that matter). Your personality, your family, the details of your journey, even the way in which you came to Him have a purpose in His economy. There are confines on this earth that have the earmarks of limitation, but only a confined attitude can hinder your effectiveness. A confined perspective is an earthly perspective; a trusting perspective is a faith-filled perspective.

You may appear to be the most unlikely person to accomplish something significant and great for the Lord. Was not Rizpah in this category? Who would have thought that a little concubine, a bit of pavement, would become a hot coal on the tip of an arrow? Who would have thought that her life would make a mark on a generation, as well as on generations to come? "God often chooses unlikely people through whom to work. He does so because there is a better chance that He will get the glory if He uses people who are nothing and have nothing going for them in the natural." [6]

If you are struggling with the confines of this earth that come through circumstances or people, challenge yourself to do some honest intro-spection. Ask yourself if your desires for promotion or a release from your situation are for God's glory or for your own. Ask yourself if your desire for personal comfort is for His testimony in you or simply for your own enjoyment. Do you care more about dying to yourself and living for Him, regardless of the cost, or more about living for yourself?

If you are in a season of young parenthood and struggling with it more than just a bit, ponder this:

Between the innocence of babyhood and the dignity of man-hood we find a delightful creature called a boy. Boys come in assorted sizes, weights, and colors, but all boys have the same creed: to enjoy every second of every minute of every hour of every day and to protest with noise (their only weapon) when their last minute is finished and the adult males pack them off to bed at night.

Boys are found everywhere—on top of, underneath, inside of, climbing on, swinging from, running around, or jumping to. Mothers love them, little girls hate them, older sisters and broth-ers tolerate them, adults ignore them, and Heaven protects them. A boy is Truth with dirt on its face, Beauty with a cut on its finger, Wisdom with bubble gum in its hair, and the Hope of the future with a frog in its pocket. [7]

A little girl can be sweeter (and badder) oftener than anyone else in the world. She can jitter around, and stomp, and make funny noises that frazzle your nerves; yet just when you open your mouth, she stands there demure with that special look in her eyes. A girl is Innocence playing in the mud, Beauty standing on its head, and Motherhood dragging a doll by the foot.

God borrows from many creatures to make a little girl. He uses the song of a bird, the squeal of a pig, the stubbornness of a mule, the antics of a monkey, the spryness of a grasshopper, the curiosity of a cat, the speed of a gazelle, the slyness of a fox, the softness of a kitten, and to top it all off He adds the mysterious mind of a woman. [8]

Do not despise the days or grow weary of the season of young parenthood. It is but a season. It will pass like tulips in the spring. Enjoy the season. Put the music on and play; sing songs off-key, on-key, in any key you can. Worship Jesus openly with infectious joy and fun. Laugh out loud and grin within; laugh in the house, around the house, and nearly everywhere you go. When there is no joy, find it; do not let joy evade you. Jump in mud puddles, chase leaves in the wind, cry when knees are scraped, and laugh when goldfish are swallowed. Crawl when there's crawling to do, run when there's running to do, and bicycle when there's bicycling to do. Chuckle when crayon markings show up on your wall or bubblegum is raggedly cut out of a toddler's hair, and discipline with the kind of love that will grow a child into an adult who will love you all the days of his or her life. Enjoy the journey of motherhood; it is but a fleeting moment.

Whether single or married, if you, like Rizpah, have realized the fulfillment of your dreams in some very major areas of life and yet you feel that your hopes for the future are narrow and hemmed-in by people, circumstances, or a season of life, renew your gratefulness for the place God has designated for you. If you, like Rizpah, are not married, but have all the responsibilities of motherhood, trust that the God of heaven is ordering your steps while He watches over you and yours. When was the last time you meditated on the obvious and not-so-obvious blessings God has placed in your life? Why is it that you have allowed circumstances or others to blind your eyes and cover your rejoicing heart with an emotionally defeating and suffocating wet blanket?

Challenge yourself to think outside the box. Think creatively about how you can accomplish His will wherever He has planted you and whatever season of life that you are in. It is only your own perspective that can truly narrow your hopes. Your faith and future hope are never limited from God's perspective. Tune in to His voice afresh if you have felt limited by the circumstances or season of life or the perspectives of others. "If we will live our lives to glorify God and not seek glory for ourselves, He will take care of making sure that we are blessed and honored. Seek to be well-known in the spiritual Kingdom—not necessarily among men." [9] Places of glory and honor belong to the Lord, not to any man or woman. We would be wise not to seek those places, but rather to remain at the feet of Jesus, seeking how our lives might please Him and count for His purposes in the earth. What a privilege it is to sit quietly in His Presence and listen to His life-giving encouragement for the journey ahead.

Have you placed your hopes in something temporal or in someone other than the living God? If you have, offer them up to God. At best, they can only offer you momentary happiness. Real joy is found in the center of His will, in the focal point of His purposes. Give these temporal offerings back to God, the Creator of all blessings. He has your best interest in mind and will faithfully lead you on the pathway of fulfillment to the Rock, Christ Jesus. His blessings will far outweigh anything this world has to offer, for His hope goes beyond the confines of this earth. Once again dream the dreams that God has for you. Let your dreams be realized and your hopes be expanded through a faith that surpasses your own understanding.

Hope in Perspective

PSALM 31:24: *"Be of good courage, and He shall strengthen your heart, All you who hope in the LORD."*

PSALM 33:18: *"Behold, the eye of the LORD is on those who fear Him, On those who hope in His mercy."*

PSALM 38:15: *"For in You, O LORD, I hope; You will hear, O Lord my God."*

PSALM 42:5: *"Why are you downcast, O my soul? Why so disturbed within me? Put your hope in God, for I will yet praise him, my Savior and my God." (NIV)*

PSALM 71:5-8: *"For you have been my hope, O Sovereign LORD, my confidence since my youth. From birth I have relied on you; you brought me forth from my mother's womb. I will ever praise you. I have become like a portent to many, but you are my strong refuge. My mouth is filled with your praise, declaring your splendor all day long." (NIV)*

PSALM 119:81: *"My soul faints with longing for your salvation, but I have put my hope in your word." (NIV)*

PSALM 119:114: *"You are my refuge and my shield; I have put my hope in your word." (NIV)*

PROVERBS 10:28: *"The hope of the righteous will be gladness, but the expectations of the wicked will perish."*

ACTS 2:26: *"Therefore my heart is glad and my tongue rejoices; my body also will live in hope." (NIV)*

1 CORINTHIANS 9:10: *"He who plows should plow in hope, and he who threshes in hope should be partaker of his hope."*

GALATIANS 5:5: *"For we through the Spirit eagerly wait for the hope of righteousness by faith."*

EPHESIANS 4:4: *"There is one body and one Spirit, just as you were called in one hope of your calling."*

COLOSSIANS 1:5: *"...because of the hope which is laid up for you in heaven..."*

COLOSSIANS 1:27: *"To them God willed to make known what are the riches of the glory of this mystery among the Gentiles: which is Christ in you, the hope of glory."*

TITUS 2:11–13: *"For the grace of God that brings salvation has appeared to all men, teaching us that, denying ungodliness and worldly lusts, we should live soberly, righteously, and godly in the present age, looking for the blessed hope and glorious appearing of our great God and Savior Jesus Christ."*

TITUS 3:7: *"That having been justified by His grace we should become heirs according to the hope of eternal life."*

HEBREWS 6:17–20: *"Thus God, determining to show more abundantly to the heirs of promise the immutability of His counsel, confirmed it by an oath, that by two immutable things, in which it is impossible for God to lie, we might have strong consolation, who have fled for refuge to lay hold of the hope set before us. This hope we have as an anchor of the soul, both sure and steadfast, and which enters the Presence behind the veil, where the forerunner has entered for us, even Jesus, having become High Priest forever according to the order of Melchizedek."*

1 PETER 1:20-21: *"He indeed was foreordained before the foundation of the world, but was manifest in these last times for you who through Him believe in God, who raised Him from the dead and gave Him glory, so that your faith and hope are in God."*

1 JOHN 3:2-3: *"Beloved, now we are children of God; and it has not yet been revealed what we shall be, but we know that when He is revealed, we shall be like Him, for we shall see Him as He is. And everyone who has this hope in Him purifies himself, just as He is pure."*

NOTES

1   Armoni (SC 764) from 759; palatial; (759) from an unused root (meaning, to be *elevated*); a *citadel* (from its *height*):— castle, palace. James Strong, S.T.D., L.L.D., *Strong's Exhaustive Concordance, Compact Edition* (Grand Rapids, MI: Baker Book House, 1978), 17.

2   "Whatever Saul's failures, amassing a harem was not among them. His wife's name was Ahinoam, and she bore him four sons that we know of (Jonathan, Abinadab, Malchishua, and Ish-bosheth) and two daughters (Merab and Michal). See 1 Samuel 14:49-50; 2 Samuel 2:8; 1 Chronicles. 8:33." Howard F. Vos, *Nelson's New Illustrated Bible Manners & Customs* (Nashville, TN: Thomas Nelson, 1999), 153.

3   Portions of 1 Samuel 2:1–2 (NIV): "Then Hannah prayed and said: 'My heart rejoices in the LORD; in the LORD my horn is lifted high. My mouth boasts over my enemies, for I delight in your deliverance. There is no one holy like the LORD; there is no one besides you; there is no Rock like our God.'"

4   This is a paraphrase of a prayer from Helen Good Brenneman, *Meditations for the New Mother* (Scottdale, PA: Herald Press, 1973), 17.

5   Mephibosheth (SC 4648) from 6284 and 1322; *dispeller of shame* (i.e. of Baal) (p. 70) (6284) a prim root; to *puff*, i.e. *blow* away:— scatter into corners (p. 93) (1322) *shame* …(put to) shame…(p. 24). James Strong, S.T.D., L.L.D., *Strong's Exhaustive Concordance, Compact Edition* (Grand Rapids, MI: Baker Book House, 1978), 70, 93, 24.

6   Joyce Meyer, *Life in the Word* (New York: Warner Books, 1998), 108.

7   Helen Good Brenneman, *Meditations for the Expectant Mother* (Scottdale, PA: Herald Press, 1973), 72.

8   Ibid., 70.

9   Meyer, *Life in the Word*, 109.

Pawn or Princess?

Seeing It God's Way

And Saul had a concubine, whose name was Rizpah, the daughter of Aiah. So Ishbosheth said to Abner, "Why have you gone in to my father's concubine?" — *2 Samuel 3:7*

Darkness engulfed her soul. She had worn a black mourning dress for so long that she could barely remember the rich hues of purple, red, and royal blue that once covered her. It seemed as though the sun would never rise again. Dark circles sagged beneath her heavy-laden eyes, and worry filled her heart. The days of the joys of young motherhood were over and gone. These were days of unending sorrow, suspicion, and treachery in the kingdom. She was not sure if her fate rested in the hands of one of Saul's sons, the commander of his armies, or the God of heaven. Was she a pawn in the kingdom of mankind, or was she the princess of God, chosen and anointed by Him for a great work on earth?

After the reports of Saul's death came to Rizpah's ears, she thought that her world would end. Much to her own surprise, she had actually grown to love him, and although she was concerned about her own demise, she was genuinely sorrowful for the loss of the father of her sons. He was the only man she had ever known intimately, and he had treated her with such tenderness and genuine care that she had given her heart and love to him in complete surrender over and over again. The love between them was different than the love between him and Ahinoam, his beloved wife, but nevertheless it was genuine and had bonded her heart to his.

Ahinoam had also been kind to her in these years. She had never once exhibited jealousy toward Rizpah; she had even helped and encouraged her on many occasions. She never treated her like many of the wives she had heard about who mistreated their husband's concubines. She had in fact become like the mother Rizpah never knew. She wasn't as wise as old Phoebe, but perhaps just as kind. Upon hearing of Saul's death and the death of her son Jonathan, Ahinoam fasted and mourned for seven days openly, then closed herself in her apartment. An overwhelming, dark depression overcame her and she died within weeks. When Rizpah heard the grievous news of her death, she once again donned her black mourning dress and wept aloud with deep groanings from within for this precious mother in Israel. Covered in black cloth and heavy of heart, her slightly graying hair looked grayer, and the sunken circles under her eyes retained pools of tears that gently cascaded down her cheeks. The memories of those days were still fresh in her mind; she could still feel the ache of sorrow as she pondered her great loss.

Then, just as the surprise report of Saul's death had come to her months before, the arrival of the commander of Saul's army on her doorstep came as a shock as well. Commander Abner was Saul's cousin, a loyal and wise leader. His very presence was commanding; his demeanor matched his commission. After Saul's fall, it was known that Abner had made Ishbosheth, Saul's younger son, king of Israel.[1] Ishbosheth was known to be weak and fearful of battle, whereas Abner was strong and fearless; and here he was on her doorstep to offer her comfort.[2] How could she help but invite him in? Although Jehovah's constant Presence had been her comfort, a human companion other than her maids and her two teen sons was indeed a welcome sight.

They spoke for hours on end for days; the days turned into weeks. He wooed her heart and brought comfort to her soul and she to his. He had been by Saul's side for nearly forty years and she for less than twenty, but they both had an unswerving love for the deceased king. Abner drew her close to himself, and the two became one in heart and in consolation. Their days together were days of peace and renewed hope for the future. Though she was somewhat apprehensive and wondered about his motivations toward her, she could not help but respond to his tranquilizing comfort. She knew that since Ahinoam's death, she was, for the first time in her life, a precious commodity in Israel; whoever might draw her and her sons into their favor could potentially have power for the future.[3]

Then just as surprisingly as Abner had appeared, the sound of the hooves of Ishbosheth's horses resounded outside her door. "What business do you have sleeping with my father's concubine?"[4] he shouted out to Abner.[5]

Angrily Abner barked back, "Treat me like a dog, will you! Is this the thanks I get for sticking by the house of your father, Saul, and all his family and friends? I personally saved you from certain capture by David, and you make an issue out of my going to bed with a woman! What God promised David, I'll help accomplish—transfer the kingdom from the house of Saul and make David ruler over the whole country, both Israel and Judah, from Dan to Beersheba. If not, may God do his worst to me."[6]

Startled by the strength and anger of Abner's outburst, Ishbosheth cowered in his presence, daring not to utter another accusation.

Rizpah shivered from head to toe hearing the angry accusations of the typically weak-willed Ishbosheth and the raging threats of Abner in return. Trembling, she crouched into the corner of her apartment, while the door hung open and the sun glared through the opening as if to expose her to the angry king's view. Tears began to fill her eyes as she felt the childhood fears of the old street corner four blocks from home come rushing back to her senses. Peace had vanished in an instant, and her old companion, terror, had returned. Were Ishbosheth's angry accusations toward Abner directed at her as well? Did he see her as manipulative and conniving? Even if Abner had meant it as a strategic ploy to overtake the throne, she had not. But if Ishbosheth presumed it to be so, what would this mean to her future?

Where were her boys? She must find them; they were no longer children, but they were not warriors yet either. What would Ishbosheth do to them if he saw them? Where was old Phoebe? Her girlhood heart needed her now. Had Abner's words of comfort been words of deceit instead? Phoebe's words had always been pure, but Abner's were indistinguishable in the intensity and loudness of this moment. Questions and thoughts were racing through her mind with flashing pictures attached to each one.

"A woman…"?

Were those the words Abner had used to describe her? "A woman…" She had heard that tone before. Just a piece of pavement, that's all she was—*a mere woman*. Nothing had changed in her life. Had she, without realizing it, put her faith in Saul and then in Abner? She knew better than to put her faith in people and things that were temporal. How could she? Petitions and frightening questions filled her mouth.

"Jehovah, am I but a pawn in a game on this earth? One minute I feel that I am Your princess, a precious daughter, and the next I realize that I am but a pawn to a king and a commander, a piece to be manipulated and moved around on a game board. Help me, Jehovah. I'm drowning in the swirling rapids of men's plots and schemes. My faith is in You, not in people, not in places, not in positions of today or tomorrow."

This hill-town of Benjamin, this "Gibeah of Saul," [7] had been surprisingly good to her over the years, but now it was a hill enshrouded by a heavy fog. It was virtually a ghost town. Kindhearted Ahinoam, the beloved wife of Saul, was gone; their sons were either dead or gone to war; and their daughters were married and gone. Saul was forever gone, his body in Jabesh Gilead somewhere. Abner was now gone and Ishbosheth was on the run. Gone, gone, gone—they were all gone. The grim realities of war had taken their toll on nearly every part of her life. All that was left were her two faithful but frightened maids, and her sons, Armoni and Mephibosheth.

Armoni and Mephibosheth were the hope of the future. They were the only ones who could lift the fog from the hill-town she had come to know and love. She may have been a pawn in man's game of war, but surely her sons were the bright hope of tomorrow. Surely even king David would see that. Everyone knew that David had never laid a hand of vengeance against Saul or his house; he would have mercy on her and her sons. Surely he would find a place for them at his table.

Yes, David would see and release the obvious potential in her sons; he would anoint them for service in his kingdom. She could almost see it—her sons in David's palace doing his bidding, being a part of uniting the kingdom once again. Once again the seeds of faith that were planted in her soul so many years before began to blossom under the sunshine of hope that remained in her heart. Then Rizpah's eyes landed upon her sons as they drew near, and her heart began to rejoice. Though she did not speak it aloud, from deep within her she cried out, "*Be grand, Armoni. Dispel the shame and wickedness of Baal, my dear Mephibosheth. Be fruitful overcomers in your generation, my sons. My faith resides in Jehovah, the everlasting God, but it sees the future in you.*"

Have you ever felt that you were going somewhere…only to find out that you weren't? Have you ever felt that you were finally going to reach the top of the proverbial ladder, only to have it pulled out from underneath you? Have you ever realized that there were people in your life who cared more about using you for their benefit than releasing you to accomplish God's will in your life? Have you ever felt like a pawn in a giant game of chess rather than a chosen, anointed servant of the Most High God?

If you've experienced these things, you must learn to see life with God's eyes. You can't look at your circumstances—they're temporary. You can't look to people—though you may be friends throughout eternity, they're temporary residents of this earth as well. You've got to see your life from His perspective, not yours, not anyone else's. God is the only One with an eternal perspective, seeing the end from the beginning. You may be a pawn in someone's strategy in life, but not in the eternal God's. You are blessed and chosen for a purpose to Him.

The realization that your earthly encouragers and protectors in life have vanished or been vanquished puts you in the "alone with God" box. That's a good place to be! One person said it this way: "Walking with God is like riding a tiger. It's dangerous to ride, but deadly to get off." [8] You can feel frightened, alone, and discouraged at times in life, but that is the time to cry out to God, not avoid Him. That's the time to ask that you might be able to see what He sees, not what you already see with your natural eyes. That's what faith is all about. It's that substance that is invisible to the natural eye.

If your Saul and Ahinoam have died and your Phoebe is a distant memory, the Holy Spirit longs to comfort you. He longs to be there for you and with you. He is the only One "who will never leave you nor forsake you." [9] If your Abner has only loved you to use you, God will "render vengeance…He will provide atonement…for…His people." [10] So continue to seek the Master, knowing that He sees all and knows all and will read your sincere trust in Him as a faith statement and will reward you for it. He is the rewarder and comforter; He is the One you can count on to be present when you need Him; He is the One who will never take advantage of you. Reach for Him in times of distress, tribulation, and loneliness. He'll be there.

If you have ever been falsely accused, let God be your defense. [11] When a person is attacking another for the sake of the attack, little can usually be said to stop the onslaught. However, "One thought to keep in mind whenever you're on the receiving end of any kind of abuse: in place of thinking (as so many do), 'What is wrong with me that he treats me like this?' think, 'What's wrong with him that he's treating me in this way.'" [12] The verbal attack likely has very little to do with you personally and has a whole lot to do with unhealed, un-dealt-with, pent-up frustration in the accuser. Refuse to succumb to a victim's posture or mentality.

When people have a low estimation of their personal value, they become easy prey for abusive people. They are susceptible to false accusations, berating, and validation of their own unworthiness. When they have a healthy realization of who they are in Christ, they may be temporarily affected by such deeds of ignorance and wickedness, but they don't stay down long before their healthy self-worth comes bounding once again to the surface of their heart.

If you have a reasonable awareness of your personal value to Christ, but are struggling due to an attack by someone you trusted with your heart, know that God is still with you. Sadly, those that abuse come in all shapes and sizes and in all kinds of relationships. They can be marriage partners, children, Christian leaders, bosses, well-meaning friends, and hurtful critics. It is paramount that you be diligent about keeping your heart clean before the Lord. The Psalmist cried out, "Create in me a clean heart, O God, and renew a steadfast spirit within me. Do not cast me away from Your presence, and do not take Your Holy Spirit from me. Restore to me the joy of Your salvation, and uphold me by Your generous Spirit." (Psalm 51:10–12)

I recommend five steps for maintaining a clean heart when it comes to hurt, misuse, and false accusations:

1. **Confess the hurt.** Be honest with yourself and with God about the hurt in your own heart. Where does it hurt and why does it hurt there?

   If we confess our sins, He is faithful and just to forgive us our sins and to cleanse us from all unrighteousness. (1 John 1:9)

   The word "sins" in this passage refers to offenses as well as sins in the original language.[13] So confess your offenses to God, give them to Him.

2. **Forgive.** Do not let any unforgivingness reside in your heart. Forgive the abusive person. Although he might be arrogant about his station in life, ignorant of his own heart issues, or simply insensitive, he likely did not purpose to hurt you by his comments or deeds.

   "Judge not, and you shall not be judged. Condemn not, and you shall not be condemned. Forgive, and you will be forgiven." (Luke 6:37)

3. **Release the hurt and the offense.** Give it to God. This is a trust issue now between you and the Creator of your heart. Only God has the right to avenge. Also never, never gossip about the offender. Receiving pastoral counsel is appropriate, but gossip will never be rewarded.

   "Beloved, do not avenge yourselves, but rather give place to wrath; for it is written, 'Vengeance is Mine, I will repay,' says the Lord." (Romans 12:19)

4. **Renew your mind through the power of prayer and the Word of God.** God is a supernatural being, and interacting with Him verbally and meditating on His Word releases encouragement and healing to the wounded soul. Both have the power to renew, refresh, and restore the mind.

   "And do not be conformed to this world, but be transformed by the renewing of your mind, that you may prove what is that good and acceptable and perfect will of God." (Romans 12:2)

5. **Move forward and choose joy.** Leave behind the past and reach forward to the future. Choose joy on a daily basis.

"Blessed are you when men hate you, and when they exclude you, and revile you, and cast out your name as evil, for the Son of Man's sake. Rejoice in that day and leap for joy! For indeed your reward is great in heaven..." (Luke 6:22–23a)

If you put these principles into daily use and find that your heart is still bruised, if you find yourself avoiding the offender or similar types of people, know that avoidance is not healthy but that tenderness and caution are both healthy and honest emotions. If you fear that you will never be the same again, you are right. You will never be the same again. You must accept that life experiences change us. This, however, is not a dismal fact. Joy will be restored to you, life will find normalcy, and there really will come a time when you'll trust again. But you will never be the same again, so don't plan on it. To be the same is simply not possible—life will change you, mold you, and shape you.

Negative life experiences affect everyone. Granted, these experiences don't "just happen." They happen by man's evil choices, by ignorance and insensitivity, by Satan's evil intent, or perhaps even by God trying to get our attention. However, they do happen. If you let it, life will change you for the better, not the worse. The experiences of life do not have power over you; you have the power over them. You have within you, through the Holy Spirit, the ability to choose how life's experiences will change and affect you.

Know that you please the Lord each day by continuing to choose to walk by His principles. Know that He is pleased with you, even if it has been a long time since you have "felt" His pleasure. Now willingly embrace the fact that you will indeed never be the same again (yes, embrace it). It's okay to lament over the loss—shed as many tears as you need to. Now determine that you will continue to choose joy daily, and confess to the Lord that you desperately need a miracle from Him. He is in the emotional healing and miracle-working business. You serve a miracle-working God.

When activating the biblical principles of confessing, forgiving, releasing, renewing, and choosing joy daily, know that your miracle is on the way!

If we could do it ourselves, we would not need faith!
We do not need faith for the possible, but for the impossible!
We do not need faith for the natural, but for the supernatural!
We do not need faith for the probable, but for the improbable!
We do not need faith for what we can do, but for what we
cannot do! [14]

If you will be faithful to work the principles of God, He will be faithful to heal your wounded heart and to not only restore you to wholeness, but to make you more than a conqueror. [15] Never believe that you are a pawn in the game of life—you are a prince or a princess, a vessel chosen by the Creator of the Universe. Go out today knowing that God is on your side and He will take care of the issues in your heart.

Cleansing and Renewing the Heart

CONFESS

PSALM 32:5: *"I acknowledged my sin to You, and my iniquity I have not hidden. I said, 'I will confess my transgressions to the LORD,' and You forgave the iniquity of my sin. Selah."*

1 JOHN 1:9: *"If we confess our sins, He is faithful and just to forgive us our sins and to cleanse us from all unrighteousness."*

PHILIPPIANS 2:11: *"Every tongue should confess that Jesus Christ is Lord, to the glory of God the Father."*

JAMES 5:16: *"Confess your trespasses to one another, and pray for one another, that you may be healed. The effective, fervent prayer of a righteous man avails much."*

FORGIVE

PSALM 86:5: *"For You, Lord, are good, and ready to forgive, And abundant in mercy to all those who call upon You."*

JEREMIAH 31:34: *"No more shall every man teach his neighbor, and every man his brother, saying, 'Know the LORD,' for they all shall know Me, from the least of them to the greatest of them, says the LORD. For I will forgive their iniquity, and their sin I will remember no more."*

MATTHEW 6:14: *"For if you forgive men their trespasses, your heavenly Father will also forgive you."*

2 CORINTHIANS 2:7: *"…so that on the contrary you should rather forgive and comfort him, otherwise such a one might be overwhelmed by excessive sorrow." (NASB)*

1 JOHN 1:9: *"If we confess our sins, He is faithful and just to forgive us our sins and to cleanse us from all unrighteousness."*

RELEASE

DEUTERONOMY 32:43: *"Rejoice, O ye nations, with his people: for he will avenge the blood of his servants, and will render vengeance to his adversaries, and will be merciful unto his land, and to his people." (KJV)*

1 SAMUEL 24:12: *"May the LORD judge between you and me, and may the LORD avenge me on you; but my hand shall not be against you." (NASB)*

ROMANS 12:19: *"Never take your own revenge, beloved, but leave room for the wrath of God, for it is written, 'VENGEANCE IS MINE, I WILL REPAY,' says the Lord." (NASB)*

RENEW

PSALM 51:10: *"Create in me a clean heart, O God; and renew a right spirit within me." (KJV)*

ISAIAH 40:31: *"But those who wait on the LORD shall renew their strength; they shall mount up with wings like eagles, they shall run and not be weary, they shall walk and not faint."*

LAMENTATIONS 5:21: *"Turn us back to You, O LORD, and we will be restored; renew our days as of old."*

ROMANS 12:2: *"And do not be conformed to this world, but be transformed by the renewing of your mind, so that you may prove what the will of God is, that which is good and acceptable and perfect." (NASB)*

TITUS 3:5: *"…not by works of righteousness which we have done, but according to His mercy He saved us, through the washing of regeneration and renewing of the Holy Spirit."*

CHOOSE JOY

PSALM 5:11: *"But let all those rejoice who put their trust in You; let them ever shout for joy, because You defend them; let those also who love Your name be joyful in You."*

PSALM 27:6: *"And now my head shall be lifted up above my enemies all around me; therefore I will offer sacrifices of joy in His tabernacle; I will sing, yes, I will sing praises to the LORD."*

PSALM 30:5: *"For His anger is but for a moment, His favor is for life; weeping may endure for a night, but joy comes in the morning."*

PSALM 51:8: *"Make me hear joy and gladness, that the bones You have broken may rejoice."*

PSALM 51:12: *"Restore to me the joy of Your salvation, and uphold me by Your generous Spirit."*

PSALM 67:4: *"Oh, let the nations be glad and sing for joy! For You shall judge the people righteously, and govern the nations on earth. Selah."*

PSALM 126:5: *"Those who sow in tears shall reap in joy."*

PROVERBS 15:23: *"A man has joy by the answer of his mouth, And a word spoken in due season, how good it is!"*

ECCLESIASTES 2:26: *"For God gives wisdom and knowledge and joy to a man who is good in His sight; but to the sinner He gives the work of gathering and collecting, that he may give to him who is good before God. This also is vanity and grasping for the wind."*

NOTES

1   "Upon the death of Saul, Abner took up the cause of the young heir to the throne, Ishbosheth, whom he forthwith removed from the neighborhood of David to Mahanaim in the East-Jordanic country. There he proclaimed him king over all Israel..." *International Standard Bible Encyclopedia;* 00340 81.03.

2   "Ishbosheth's known weakness, which accounts for his absence from the battle of Gilboa, suited well Abner's ambition." *Fausset's Bible Dictionary; Bible Works;* 00099 46 Abner; 00100 46.01.

3   "Abner had certainly perceived the utter incapacity of Ishbosheth for a very long time, ... and had probably made him king after the death of Saul, merely that he might save himself,...and might be able to rule in Ishbosheth's name, and possibly succeed in paving his own way to the throne. His appropriation of the concubine of the deceased monarch was at any rate a proof according to Israelitish notions,...that he was aiming at the throne..." *Keil and Delitzsch Commentary on the Old Testament;* E-Sword; 2 Sa 3:6-39.

4   Quote from Eugene Peterson, *The Message//Remix: The Bible in Contemporary Language* (Colorado Springs, CO: NavPress, 2003), 514.

5   "Whether Abner was really guilty of this sin or not is not easy to determine; though, by his not absolutely denying it, it looks as if it was not merely a jealousy of Ishbosheth, or a false report made unto him; though, especially if he was not fully satisfied of it, it would have been his wisdom to have said nothing of it to him, since his continuance on the throne so much depended on him." *John Gill's Exposition of the Entire Bible;* E-Sword; 2 Sa 3:7

6   Eugene Peterson, *The Message//Remix,* 514.

7   "Gibeah, a hill or hill-town, "of Benjamin" 1 Sa 13:15 better known as "Gibeah of Saul" 1 Sa 11:4; Isa. 10:29. It was here that the terrible outrage was committed on the Levite's concubine which led to the almost utter extirpation of the tribe of Benjamin...this was the birthplace of Saul, and continued to be his residence after he became king. 1 Sa 10:26; 11:4; 15:34." *Easton's Bible Dictionary; Bible Works;* 01476.

8   Originator of this quote is unknown.

9   "Let your conduct be without covetousness; be content with such things as you have. For He Himself has said, 'I will never leave you nor forsake you.'" (Hebrews 13:5)

10 "Rejoice, O Gentiles, with His people; for He will avenge the blood of His servants, and render vengeance to His adversaries; He will provide atonement for His land and His people." (Deuteronomy 32:43)

11 "I will wait for You, O You his Strength; for God is my defense." (Psalm 59:9)

12 Gary J. Oliver, PhD, and H. Norman Wright, *Good Women Get Angry: A Woman's Guide to Handling Anger, Depression, Anxiety and Stress* (Ann Arbor, MI: Servant Publications, 1995), 193.

13 "266 hamartia, *ham-ar-tee'-ah;* from 264; sin (prop.abstr.):-- offence, sin(-ful). James Strong, *Strong's Exhaustive Concordance, Complete and unabridged, Compact Edition with dictionaries of Hebrew and Greek words* (Grand Rapids, MI: Baker Book House, 1978), 10.

14. Wendell Smith, *Great Faith, Making God Big* (Portland, OR: City Bible Publishing, 2001), 30.

15. "Yet in all these things we are more than conquerors through Him who loved us." (Romans 8:37)

Faith's Call to Sacrifice

Requirements of Faith

Costly Obedience

Now there was a famine in the days of David for three years, year after year; and David inquired of the LORD. And the LORD answered.... Therefore David said to the Gibeonites, "...With what shall I make atonement...?" "Let seven men of his descendants be delivered to us, and we will hang them before the LORD in Gibeah of Saul, whom the LORD chose." And the king said, "I will give them." — 2 Samuel 21:1, 3, 6

Sitting near her doorway in the last bit of shade that would be afforded her for the rest of the afternoon, Rizpah enjoyed the momentary quiet. The afternoon heat was stifling, but a gentle breeze came over the hilltop and cooled her brow. This faithful, soothing breeze seemed to find its way to her each day as if it was the very breath of God come to refresh her. She so enjoyed these afternoon moments of repose. They always gave her the opportunity to focus her mind on the goodness of Jehovah rather than on the rumors that continued to come to the palace grounds from the neighboring communities below.

She didn't place much stock in the rumors nowadays. What did the people of the land know of kings and commanders? What did they know of the gods of famine or the judgments of Jehovah? She could not focus on such frivolous tales. When such tales tried to overcome her spirit, she pushed them away with praises to a living God who had remained ever close to her and her sons. Though the heat was suffocating at times, she could always find a bit of shade and that faithful gentle breeze. Though the food portions were meager and had to be parceled out, there was somehow always enough. Though there were continual reasons to be anxious, she had a joy-filled faith in her heart that could not be stopped.

Most obvious of all, though there were no more kings or commanders around, she had her beloved sons at her beck and call to comfort her and bring her joy. How she loved to watch Armoni practice with the sword and do hand-to-hand combat with the agile sons of some of the resident servants. He carried himself with a strong and commanding presence like his father Saul. He was every bit as tall as Saul, with curly black hair and flashing black eyes. She had confidence that when king David met him one day, Armoni would find favor in the king's eyes as a potential leader in his army. *Skill yourself with strength and with wisdom, my son, for the kings of this earth look well upon those such as you.*

Mephibosheth, on the other hand, was a continual student of the Law of Moses. Unlike Armoni, he was fairer in skin tone and not as tall, yet tall enough. He was equally as handsome, with piercing green eyes that could look straight through the windows of your soul on any given day. He was a kind, intelligent, and compassionate young man. She loved to watch him pore over the ancient scrolls in Saul's library and listen to him pontificate about his insights to her and Armoni over their morsels of food in the early evening. He was developing such wisdom that she was continually amazed at his knowledge and understanding. Perhaps he would be her next mentor rather than she his. *Learn your lessons well, my son, for Jehovah yearns to whisper the secrets of heaven within your hearing.*

Yes, although there was famine in the land and her natural security no longer existed, Rizpah found peace in Jehovah and delight in her sons. They were the hope of the future, and she rejoiced at the wonder of what amazing men of God they had both become. Her daily pondering of the wonders of Jehovah and the joy of her two sons now shifted to King David. Though Saul had hated him with fiery contempt, she had only heard good reports of David from others throughout the years. At times, when Saul would return home with blistering curses regarding David, her servants gave her reports through his soldiers of how David had spared him and would not lay a hand on God's anointed king. He had never harmed Saul, and he had never extended the arm of battle to her or her sons.

She wondered about this man David and how he was faring in his role as king. From a distance it seemed as though nothing had gone well for him in these past three years. The famine was increasingly severe and the people were looking to him for answers. Intercession filled her heart. *"Jehovah, bless this king with Your insight and wisdom. Give him the ability to hear Your direction and the courage to do Your bidding. Set Your people free from this famine; let rains of refreshing fall once again upon the land. Bless Your servant David. Have mercy upon him as You have had mercy upon me and mine."* Nearly asleep now in the lull of the mid-afternoon heat, she imagined David sitting in his cedar palace under the same beating sun.

The fragrance of cedar filled his nostrils as the temperature rose and the afternoon sun penetrated his home.[1] When the summer heat was upon his palace, the rich and comforting aroma always filled his home. It reminded him of the kindness of Hiram, king of Tyre, and his generosity toward him in building his home there in Jerusalem.[2] The aroma was soothing to David for that very reason, as it represented not only the generosity of Hiram, but also the generosity of the Lord toward him. Reclining on his elbow and taking in the fragrance of the wood, King David pondered the agonizing drought and the ways of the Lord as his servant slowly lifted and then lowered the great palm in his hands. The motion was meant to create a gentle breeze that could cool the rising temperature of the afternoon hour from his master's furrowed brow, but no matter how often David felt the wafting of the gentle breeze, it was only a breath of hot, sultry air in motion. It neither cooled nor refreshed him. Was the famine never going to abate? Was there not a solution from heaven to be heard?

As he looked at the table before him, he could see that there was nothing sumptuous about the food in front of him. It was simply flatbread, goat's cheese, and leathery meat from a starving calf. Precious few fattened calves were left in the kingdom after three long years of famine. David's taste buds longed for luscious grapes and pomegranates, but neither the vines nor the small trees had leafed and produced any succulent fruit for a long time.

Both the heat and humidity were rising as the afternoon lingered. If only it were possible, David would reach for a knife and cut through the heavy heat, releasing the rains of heaven upon the land and upon his people. Even in the midst of the rising heat however, David felt stirred not to allow his spirit to dry out like the vineyards and groves. He requested of his servant to bring him a clean tunic and then told him to take leave and to tell the guards outside his door to make sure that no one disturbed him.[3] He cried out to Jehovah filling his mouth with petitions of need and proclamations of faith,

"Oh Sovereign One, I cry out to You; You are my rock and my fortress; You are my deliverer; the God of my strength. It is in You that I trust. You are my shield and the horn of my salvation. You are my stronghold and my refuge, my Savior in battle. I call upon You; You alone are worthy to be praised. With the merciful You will show Yourself merciful. With the pure You will show Yourself pure; You will save your people who have been humbled by this drought.

You are my lamp, O Lord; enlighten my eyes to see Your will. Anoint my ears to hear Your voice. I know that Your way is perfect, for Your word is proven. You are a shield to all who trust You, and I do trust You with all my being.

Who is a rock, except my God?[4] God, You are my strength and power; You make my way perfect. God, show me the way of deliver-

ance for Your people. I am inquiring of You and You alone. Speak to me Lord; I am listening. Whatever You say, I will obey. Whatever sacrifice You require, I will offer. Please, come and pour rains of refreshing upon the land and upon Your people."

As David now lay prostrate before the Lord on the stone floor of his palace apartment, he tuned his ear to listen to the voice of the Lord. He rarely needed a shout from Jehovah in moments like these—a conversational tone between two friends was all his heart yearned for. Just to hear the voice of Jehovah, his mighty God and faithful Friend, just one word of instruction and deliverance from this overwhelming drought, was all he needed to hear; that word alone would bring refreshing.

His soul ached both day and night with the burden of a shepherd's heart and the weight of a king's responsibility. David cared little for his own frivolous desires for grapes and pomegranates What his heart truly longed for was to see the land restored to fruitfulness and the people of God to health and prosperity. Once again he cried out from the depths of his soul, *"Why, Lord? Why does this drought not end? I beg of You; let the rains fall, the land be restored, and the people be renewed. My heart and soul inquires of You. Speak to me, Lord. I, Your servant, am listening. Whatever You say, I will obey. No sacrifice is too great for You or for Your people, Whatever you require, I will offer. Speak to Your servant, O Most High. I am listening."*

Then, just as a gracious and faithful mentor would calmly enter a room in an atmosphere of quiet learning, the voice of the Lord spoke clearly and openly in David's hearing. "It is because of Saul and his bloodthirsty house, because he killed the Gibeonites."[5] The revelation had come; David did not need another word. God had spoken clearly and succinctly. His spirit received the instruction of the Lord.

Even though he knew that the Gibeonites had deceived Joshua into making a treaty with him rather than annihilating them four centuries ago, he also knew that Jehovah was a covenant-keeping God. To Him, an oath was an oath of promise never to be broken, and Saul had violated that oath with an ego-laden vengeance. In his zeal for the honor of Israel and Judah, as well as for his own name, he had attempted to utterly destroy the Gibeonites. Even after four hundred years, Jehovah had not forgotten the promise of his faithful leader Joshua to this people, and now David must see to it that the Gibeonites were requited so that the newly united kingdom of Israel might experience the blessing of the Lord once again.

Now raising to his knees with his hands lifted to heaven David proclaimed, "Blessed be the LORD, because He has heard the voice of my supplications! The LORD is my strength and my shield; My heart trusted in Him, and I am helped; therefore my heart greatly rejoices." [6] Standing, he called to the guards to send for his messenger. He then sent his servant with an urgent dispatch asking a delegation of the Gibeonites to come at once to have audience with him.

Upon their arrival, David had his servants wash their feet, anoint their heads with oil, and offer them a feast of leg of lamb, flatbread, goat's cheese, and a cooling drink for their palates. He then spoke with them of Saul's regretful bloodthirsty attempt to annihilate their people: "For four centuries the Israelites have been at peace with your people. Then Saul and his company violated the oath that our predecessor Joshua made with your nation so long ago. Jehovah does not forget oaths, and famine has been upon our land for three years now because of Saul's sin against you. What can I do for you? How can I compensate you so that you will bless God's legacy of land and people?" [7]

The Gibeonite delegation replied, "We don't want any money from Saul and his family. And it's not up to us to put anyone in Israel to death." But David persisted: "What are you saying I should do for you?" Then they told the king, "The man who tried to get rid of us, who schemed to wipe us off the map of Israel—well, let seven of his sons be handed over to us to be executed—hanged before God at Gibeah of Saul, the holy mountain." And David agreed, "I'll hand them over to you." [8]

As the Gibeonites left the meeting hall, the words that had been spoken reverberated in David's mind. He knew that the compensatory payment would be high, but money or land would have been easier than the cost of life. Blood for blood was to be the payment. Even though his house would be spared and the nation as a whole would be restored, still the pain of the loss of life—any life—was agonizing to the heart of this shepherd king. He had never laid a hand on Saul, and he regretted having to raise a hand against his seed. In his head, David knew that to obey would bring blessing to the nation and restore the honor of God's covenant-keeping word, but the dread of losing any more life on Saul's account brought sorrow to his heart.

Obedience was costly, but it was a requirement of faith. His obedience would demonstrate to the people the importance of implicit obedience, that God never forgets His promises. What He says, He will do. David's obedience would also restore the waning faith of a people in a long season of drought, to a deepening trust in Jehovah God and His desire to bless. Yes, David knew that his obedience, though costly, was a requirement of renewed faith in the hearts of the people.

Obedience is faith's requirement. It is an issue of the will, and is intrinsically tied to miracle-working prayer. Obedience was an issue for David. It was for Saul, and it is for you as well. If God knew that His solution would release the miracle that was needed but that David would not obey what He asked, why would He be motivated to grant him the knowledge of His will? God does not waste words. He does not make promises that He does not keep, and He does not spend time speaking words into self-important or unheeding ears.

If David weren't in a posture of surrender and trust, on what premise would he believe that he could even hear from God? For that matter, why would he even bother to ask God for the knowledge of His will if he knew he would not follow it if it wasn't to his liking? It's amazing to think how many people seek the knowledge of God's will, all the while never intending to obey unless it suits them. God does not speak easily into these ears, for judgment goes to those who hear but do not obey. David did not have closed ears and a hardened heart. He had open ears and a surrendered heart.

How you feel about God's will and direction cannot determine your obedience. I do not believe that David delighted in the knowledge that he was going to be responsible for the ending of seven lives, even if they were the descendants of Saul. If you are going to be partially responsible for the ending of another person's life, it would serve you well to live a surrendered life unto God, knowing that you are acting in accordance with His will throughout your day. This would apply to policemen, doctors, hospital administrators, lawyers, jurors, politicians, and voters and nonvoters alike. Driving a car while sleepy or intoxicated puts the lives of people in your hands, as do playing physical contact sports, hunting with a gun, and a variety of other "things we do." Actually, the lives of individuals rest in your hands every day, whether you realize it or not. You may not be a king or a president, but you do affect the lives of those around you for eternity. If your faith is saturated with obedience no matter what the cost, your obedience will be rewarded with the knowledge of His will and the faith to walk it out. Your obedience must not be contingent upon your feelings or your ego; it must be dependent upon the will of the Father.

If God knows that your will is not surrendered to Him, He often will not entrust you with the knowledge of His will, for your sake as well as for others'. When you ask for direction, according to His will, it is then that you will know that He hears you and will answer accordingly. You can only know how to ask in accordance with His will if you are walking in accordance with His will. If you make your petitions known to Him from a posture of surrender, then you can have confidence that His Holy Spirit will teach you how to pray according to His will. First John 5:14–15 says, "Now this is the confidence that we have in Him, that if we ask anything according to His will, He hears us. And if we know that He hears us, whatever we ask, we know that we have the petitions that we have asked of Him."

Are you willing to obey God? If you are, then you are ready to receive the knowledge of His will, and it is this knowledge that will give you faith to believe for the seemingly impossible. When you have the knowledge of His will and the surrendered heart to obey it, then whether you understand it or not, your faith will believe for the God-ordained outcome.

A surrendered heart is the platform of prayer that releases faith. It is the foundation stone of faith. Utter submission to God's will opens the spiritual ear and releases faith. When a heart is in right alignment with God, it is easy to ask in faith, knowing that your petition has been heard and that an answer is on the way. "Obedience, moreover, is faith in action, and is the outflow as it is the very test of love." [9] John 14:15 says, "If you love Me, keep My commandments." If you are aligned with His will out of love, there is an incredible mutual trust, and out of that, faith grows and is released.

Obedience gives the heart the courage to believe. Obedience gives people the faith to believe that their prayers are being heard because they are in right alignment with the Father. It releases the faith to believe that He hears and answers, because you know that you please His heart with your submission to His will. It's not that your obedience earns a certain answer from God, but rather that obedience stirs faith in the heart of the believer, knowing that God is delighted to answer one who is delighted to do something with His answer. Faith cannot help but burst forth from an obedient heart.

When you are more consumed with His will than with your own, you are set free from frustration, confusion, and the need to "figure it all out." You are released to live responsibly and completely in accordance with the knowledge of His will and principles. That, in turn, releases you to walk in faith. Walking in obedience to the knowledge of His will is so freeing. It is as though nothing can harm you and everything and every circumstance in your pathway will serve God's purposes through you. An obedient heart is a free and joyful heart, even in the midst of trials. I do not believe that David was happy about ending seven lives, but I do believe that he was joyful about knowing God's will and obeying it so that rains of refreshing could once again come upon his nation.

I do not believe that God wanted to slay seven young men, but His Word is above all. His covenant promises are to be kept. When Saul violated God's promise to the Gibeonites, He violated a four-century-old covenant, and God was obligated to right the wrong. He had those young men in mind. He was the only One who knew the end from the beginning of their lives. He was the only One who could be trusted to work out His will for them and make their lives count for eternity.

Even though Saul was a covenant-breaker, God was not. He would restore His covenant promise to the Gibeonites and make the lives of Rizpah's offspring count as well. But to do all this, He needed to find a willing and faithful servant, one He could trust to carry out His Word in detail. God is a God of the details. For the lives of Rizpah's sons to hit the mark, for her story to be told throughout the ages, there needed to be a servant who would carry out God's Word perfectly. He knew He had that faithful servant in David, so it was with David He entrusted His instructions. "Faith, in its highest form, is the attitude, as well as the act, of a soul surrendered to God..." [10]

Will God find a faithful servant, a surrendered soul, in you? Can He entrust challenging, humanly perplexing, and important directives to you? Will you be a faithful, obedient servant of the Most High God? Are you an obedient listener? Are you a "doer" of God's Word or a "hearer" only? His Word is His written will and testament for you. You can practice hearing and obeying His voice by obeying the Bible, the obvious will of God. Actually, this "practice" is not really practice at all; it's obedience to His Word and is pleasing to the Lord. If you consistently read and obey the Bible, then perhaps God will whisper some specific directives to you to obey on a daily basis. Note, however, that these specific directives, if they are from Him, will always align themselves with the already written principles in the Word of God.

People who do not obey the principles of God's Word that are plainly written in the Bible tend to hear inconsistent voices and do contradictory things. Determined to be a special and unique vessel of the Lord, they spend precious little time in His Word and fail to walk out the plain truth of God. To put it plainly, they get weird. Don't do that! Enough people in the world are already doing strange things in the name of Christ—there's no need for more. Simply be faithful to God's Word, walking out His clear principles, and He will entrust you with more in the days ahead as He tunes your ear and matures your faith. Your faith will grow as you learn and obey the Word of God and as you sit in the Master's presence, listening to His voice and obeying what you hear. You must be faithful to obey His Word; then you will have full confidence that you are pleasing Him.

If you ever hear anything that is contrary to the principles of His Word, you can be sure that it is not the voice of God. Your human nature, your sin nature if I dare say so, may lead you to "hear" directives that are comfortable to your soul but contrary to His principles. God will never tell you to do anything that is contrary to His will. That's why it is so important for you to know His Word, His very plain, obvious will. Saul may have thought that God wanted him to enlarge the Israelite kingdom by doing away with the Gibeonites, but he missed God's will by not adhering to the previously promised covenant that was their protection. It was not naïve ignorance but Saul's own pride that led him down the pathway of deception and disobedience. Pride of self, in fact, opens the doorway of deception. God will never tell you to do anything that is contrary to His Word or that is meant to bring glory to yourself. He will honor you for your obedience, but the glory belongs to Him. First John 3:22 says, "Whatever we ask we receive from Him, because we keep His commandments and do those things that are pleasing in His sight." What does one have to glory about? What each of us receives, we receive from Him. Our boast should be in Him alone. All praise belongs to the Lord of the universe. We are His delight and He is ours.

Have you ever observed a toddler at play who has noticed the delighted attention of the parent looking on? Typically, children look for the approval and pleasure of an observing parent. When a toddler knows that what he or she is doing pleases the parent, the faith to play more freely increases. Their joy increases as the pleasure in the parent's eyes increase, and then the giggles of delight begin. Before you know it, delightful laughter is filling the room. The same is true with us. He delights in us, and we look for His approval and pleasure. When you know that you have heard His Word and obeyed His Voice, just as with the child, pleasure fills the air.

Obedience is costly and is not always a delight to the human soul, but it is the pleasure of the heavenly Father. It is in the Master's smile that your heart will find faith tucked away. It is there that you will find fruitfulness and fulfillment. Isaiah 1:19 says, "If you are willing and obedient, you shall eat the good of the land." Yes, obedience is faith's requirement, but it is its crown as well.

Costly and Fruitbearing Obedience

GENESIS 22:18: *"In your seed all the nations of the earth shall be blessed, because you have obeyed My voice."*

ISAIAH 1:19: *"If you are willing and obedient, you shall eat the good of the land."*

2 CORINTHIANS 10:4–6: *"For the weapons of our warfare are not carnal but mighty in God for pulling down strongholds, casting down arguments and every high thing that exalts itself against the knowledge of God, bringing every thought into captivity to the obedience of Christ, and being ready to punish all disobedience when your obedience is fulfilled."*

JAMES 1:21–25: *"Therefore lay aside all filthiness and overflow of wickedness, and receive with meekness the implanted word, which is able to save your souls. But be doers of the word, and not hearers only, deceiving yourselves. For if anyone is a hearer of the word and not a doer, he is like a man observing his natural face in a mirror; for he observes himself, goes away, and immediately forgets what kind of man he was. But he who looks into the perfect law of liberty and continues in it, and is not a forgetful hearer but a doer of the work, this one will be blessed in what he does."*

HEBREWS 11:8: *"By faith Abraham obeyed when he was called to go out to the place which he would receive as an inheritance. And he went out, not knowing where he was going."*

1 PETER 1:22: *"Since you have purified your souls in obeying the truth through the Spirit in sincere love of the brethren, love one another fervently with a pure heart."*

ROMANS 5:19: *"For as by one man's disobedience many were made sinners, so also by one Man's obedience many will be made righteous."*

HEBREWS 5:8: *"Though He was a Son, yet He learned obedience by the things which He suffered."*

PHILIPPIANS 2:8: *"And being found in appearance as a man, He humbled Himself and became obedient to the point of death, even the death of the cross."*

NOTES

1   "During this time, Hiram, king of Tyre, undoubtedly saw the wisdom of befriending David and sent him cedars to build his house in Jerusalem (2 Sam. 5:22,23, 17-25; 8:1; 21:15-22; 1 Chron. 11:15-19; 12:8-15; 14:1,2,8-17; 20:4-8)." General Editor Merrill C. Tenney, *The Zondervan Pictorial Encyclopedia of the Bible; Volume Two D-G* (Grand Rapids, MI: Zondervan, date), 36.

2   "Rulers of that part of the world used the palace as a government building. David was no exception. What his palace looked like or how large it was we do not know, but apparently it was built of cut stone with interior cedar paneling (2 Samuel 7:2). Phoenician craftsmen provided the construction skills (2 Samuel 5:11). Howard F. Vos, *Nelson's New Illustrated Bible Manners & Customs* (Nashville, TN: Thomas Nelson Publishers, 1999), 157. "In the days of the great Hiram of Tyre, Hebrews and Tyrians worked closely together in several ventures. Hiram's thirty-four-year reign overlapped that of David and Solomon. Hiram sent cedar trees, carpenters, and masons to Jerusalem to build David's palace (2 Samuel 5:11; 7:2). Later David obtained cedar wood from Tyre for building the temple." Ibid., 158.

3   "126... This was considered a necessary preparation for meeting Jehovah.... 'No man can go to the temple wearing a dirty cloth: he must either put on a clean one, or go himself to a tank and wash it, if it be soiled; or he must put on one which is quite new. Near the temples men may be often seen washing their clothes, in order to prepare themselves for some religious ceremony.'" James M. Freeman, *Manners and Customs of the Bible* (Plainfield, NJ: Logos International, 1972), 68.

"821....was a tunic or inner garment which was worn next to the skin. It usually had sleeves, and generally reached to the knees, though sometimes to the ankles." Ibid., 436.

4   This is a paraphrase of 2 Samuel 22:1–4, 26–27, 29–31, 32.

5   "Now there was a famine in the days of David for three years, year after year; and David inquired of the Lord. And the LORD answered, 'It is because of Saul and his bloodthirsty house, because he killed the Gibeonites.'" (2 Samuel 21:1)

6   "Blessed be the LORD, because He has heard the voice of my supplications! The LORD is my strength and my shield; my heart trusted in Him, and I am helped; therefore my heart greatly rejoices. And with my song I will praise Him." (Psalm 28:6–7)

7   2 Samuel 21:3, *The Message*.

8   2 Samuel 21:4-6, *The Message*.

9   E. M. Bounds, *The Complete Works of E. M. Bounds on Prayer* (Grand Rapids, MI: Baker Books, 1990), 52.

10   Ibid., 59.

The Sacrifice Required

Grief and Faith—Strange Companions

We will hang them before the LORD.... So the king took Armoni and Mephibosheth, the two sons of Rizpah the daughter of Aiah, whom she bore to Saul, and the five sons of Michal the daughter of Saul...and he delivered them into the hands of the Gibeonites, and they hanged them on the hill before the LORD. So they fell, all seven together, and were put to death. — 2 Samuel 21:6, 8–9

Her countenance revealed more of a fevered brow than a feminine glow. With the heat rising once again, the perspiration beads on Rizpah's forehead began to trickle down the sides of her face as she paced back and forth. The midnight blue covering on her head fell with each quick turn she made, and without thinking she pushed it back on each time. Though the covering caused her body heat to rise several degrees, it was proper for her to have it on when she was outside her palace apartment. She was accustomed to it; it was second nature for her hand to be continually fidgeting with the covering when she was outside. She preferred the fidgeting and fresh outdoor air to the suffocating stillness in her apartment most days anyway.

Rather than looking for a bit of shade in front of her apartment, today she would pace. She loved to pace and pray, pray and pace. She was one who had a "walking-talking" relationship with Jehovah. She, in fact, had a well-worn path on the back side of the palace grounds where she normally had her morning conversations with Jehovah. He created her and knew her ways, and she knew He didn't mind talking with her at this tempo or in this manner. She could usually think and express herself better as she walked and talked. Countless mornings and mid-afternoons, she took pause and sat under the nearby mulberry tree or in a bit of shade in front of her apartment. She loved to just ponder the ways of the Lord and the goodness of His deeds, but she'd already done that early in the morning and this was now afternoon. Her peaceful morning meditations were history and her mid-afternoon frustrations spewed from her spirit.

The heat was already stifling, nearly suffocating in fact. The breeze she created from her quickened pace cooled her a bit, even though her heart raced and perspiration trickled down her back as well as her face now. The hem of her garment flapped in the air with each quick turn she made, and she began to flail her hands in the air as she boldly expressed her frustration to the startled birds of the air.

"Rumors, rumors. I'm sick of hearing rumors! Is there no good news left in Israel? First, the rumors of Saul…who knows what really happened there? I cannot imagine my king and my lord committing suicide, but neither can I imagine him allowing an Amalekite to slay him either. I know his moods could be dark and his valleys low, but to end his life? What am I to think? It's been over three years and I'm sure that my king is lost to me now, but how? And where is his body? Is there no honor left for a fallen king in this war-torn nation?!"

"And now these new rumors have come over the hillside with the haste of a hunted doe. Will they ever stop? Even though the vista of Gibeah lay before me and I can see for miles around, this bold yet humble question pounds within my heart: "Is there a mountaintop to be seen after being in this spiritual valley for so long?" Jehovah, what am I to do? What am I to think?"

Rumors had come to the hillsides of Gibeah that Abner had been slain by Joab, the commander of David's army. It was known that this was Joab's retribution for Abner's slaying of his brother Asahel. In reaction to Ishbosheth's accusation of treason, Abner had departed Gibeah and went about persuading the northern ten tribes of Israel to unite with David, and upon David's request he restored his wife Michal back to him. Even though Abner had been well received by king David for his good deeds and powers of persuasion, Joab still despised him. When he left David, Joab sent a message for him to return. Upon doing so, Joab and his remaining brother Abishai called Abner aside to speak with him and murdered him to avenge their brother's death.

With Saul and Ahinoam and all of their sons gone, only a few were left on the palace grounds. Though Rizpah could usually discern the Lord's voice clearly, the distress of feeling so alone and being encompassed by rumors overwhelmed her. Fearing what might come upon her and her sons, Rizpah ran with her sons in tow down the hillside and back to the streets of her childhood to find her old mentor Phoebe. Surely Phoebe would remember her and have some wisdom to offer her. She searched for days, describing her to passersby and asking in the marketplace. No one had seen the old woman for many years. Then finally she came upon a hunched over old man mentoring a young beggar boy at the very spot that she and Phoebe had shared lunch and mentoring moments so many years before. It warmed her heart to see such a tradition continuing on, for the dirty-faced young boy had that old familiar look of hunger and emotional deprivation that she had when she sat on that same corner.

Entreating apologetically, Rizpah asked the old man if he knew of the old matron Phoebe. Much to her delight, he believed that she was yet alive, living just three blocks over and one block down to the right. Rizpah nearly skipped down the street as her sons, though nearly adults now, looked wide-eyed at all the beggars on the street corners. This was their first viewing of such a sight. They had grown up on the hillsides of Gibeah and never been to the city to observe the "sights." They had never seen such poverty. She felt embarrassed for the beggars as her sons stared in both naiveté and pity, and she felt ashamed that she had never told them of their mother's roots.

Although they knew she was but a concubine, she had filled them with such vision and adherence to the royal blood that flowed in their veins that they barely realized they were anything less than king's sons. When Armoni and Mephibosheth were old enough to be aware of their surroundings, Saul's children by his wife were all old enough to be off to war or married. So they easily embraced their royal roots and were proud to be sons of Saul. Armoni fully intended to be elevated to a high position one day in the kingdom, and Mephibosheth was an industrious student of the Law of Moses and was exhilarated by the idea of exposing the shame of Baal worship throughout the nation. Both her sons had been mentored by her side in the ways of wisdom and were prepared to take their rightful place when the time came. Old Phoebe would be proud of her and how she had tutored her sons in the ways of Jehovah.

They came upon the small home that the old man had described. The door was open, and Rizpah carefully walked in singing out a greeting to old Phoebe. The old woman, well advanced in years and nearly blind, reached out a wrinkled but loving hand to Rizpah as she drew near. Armoni and Mephibosheth waited near the door.

Phoebe immediately recognized Rizpah, even though she spoke not a word. With kindness in her smile but the smell of imminent death upon her, she grasped Rizpah's hand and spoke to her in loving tones. Instinctively, Rizpah knelt by her bedside while dear old Phoebe gently placed her right hand, the hand of blessing, upon her head. "Rizpah, my darling girl, I have awaited your return. Days of darkness are upon you, but the light of Jehovah goes before you. That which you have been crying out for will be yours, but in ways different than you planned or imagined."

Stroking her face and taking Rizpah's chin in her hand, with tenderness Phoebe said, "Jehovah's ways are higher than your ways. You must not question, but rather stand strong, for Jehovah is with you and will be by your side."

Tears began to fill Rizpah's eyes as she bowed her head on the edge of Phoebe's bedside.

Phoebe's hand rested now on Rizpah's head with seeming purpose as she took in a slow but shallow breath and continued "Your hope will be found on a rock. Though your sacrifice will be great, know that no sacrifice goes unnoticed by Jehovah, the Rock of your salvation."

With tears now filling her eyes as well, she took another slow breath. "The Most High God goes before you and prepares the way. He will be with you and watch over you. He will comfort you and hear your cry. He will answer your prayers and the prayers of generations to come. Return to your home, my dear Rizpah, and prepare yourself for the journey ahead. Do not fear—you will hit the mark designed for you." With ragged breath and a soft voice, she spoke her final words: "Go, my daughter. You know the way of wisdom. Call upon the All Wise One. Jehovah will be with you."

With an endearing look, Phoebe's hand slipped from Rizpah's head to her bedside, and she breathed her last.

Rizpah wept with tears of stunned awe at what had just occurred. She was sorrowful and yet at peace. The Presence of Jehovah was so close; she felt that if she reached out, she could touch His hand. Her dear old mentor had spoken a final word to her heart while He had engraved it on her soul. It was as though Jehovah Himself was speaking directly to her. She could barely drink in the wonder of it all. It was a great mystery of the blending of grief and faith; it was as though through Phoebe's hand she had placed a mantle, an anointing, upon her. What strange companions these were—grief and faith. She wondered what exactly was about to occur in the ensuing days, and yet she felt no remaining anxiety. Her spirit was at peace.

While Rizpah was lost in thought, a nursemaid that she had not noticed before stepped from a corner in the room and embraced dear old Phoebe one more time as tears flowed from her eyes. As she lifted her eyes from the deceased, she thanked Rizpah for coming and told her that Phoebe had spoken of her often lately and was holding onto each day of life waiting for her return. Phoebe had told her many times that she had a very important message to give to the concubine of Saul, her daughter of the street and Jehovah's sweet child. Rizpah and the young nursemaid wept in each other's arms at the loss of one so dear, and yet rejoiced somehow knowing that they would meet her again one day at the portals of heaven.

Upon Phoebe's word, Rizpah and her sons, Armoni and Mephibosheth, headed back toward the hills of Gibeah. She was not sure what the journey ahead entailed, but she was sure that Jehovah was with her. Even though there was no Saul, no Ahinoam, no Abner, no Phoebe, nor anyone really, Rizpah knew that Jehovah was going before her and that He would be with her. He would guide her. She could feel the impending clouds of doom gathering overhead, and yet there was a faith and strength in her heart like she had never felt before. It began to infuse her sons as well as they traveled the road toward home. She began to speak words of faith to them, reminding them of their calling to make a difference in their generation. She reminded them that with every calling, sacrifice was required.

When they arrived home, all the palace servants were anxious and worried. They were fretting over the rumors that had been coming from the hills since she had left. Her two closest confidantes and maids told her that she and her sons should turn and leave, that disaster was upon them all if they didn't. They had received word concerning king David's deliberations with the Gibeonites and heard that David's men were on their way to turn the sons of Saul over into the hands of the Gibeonites. Before they could finish giving Rizpah a full report, the sound of horses' hooves resounded in the courtyard. It was a small regiment of David's men, but they were obviously trained and skilled for what they were about to do. Behind their company, encircling the "criminals" who had committed no crimes, was a band of Gibeonites.

Tethered by their hands and riding upon five horses in the middle of the soldiers were the five sons of Merab, Saul's daughter. She had died giving birth to her fifth son, and their aunt Michal, David's first wife, had raised them to be the excellent young men they were. Now that Michal had been taken from her husband, Phaltiel, and given back to David, they had no one from the house of Saul to speak on their behalf.

Now the soldiers demanded that Rizpah's two sons be brought from her apartment and tethered by the hands and mounted onto the last two horses. Stunned, Rizpah screamed, "No! Let it not be so!"

At that moment, Armoni was struck with the fists of his captor, and Mephibosheth was slashed across the back with a whip, both being immediately tied by the wrists and then thrust onto the backs of the remaining two horses at the rear of the military troop. Rizpah fell to her knees with her hands reaching out toward her sons, tears streaming down her face.

The soldiers mounted their horses after securing Armoni and Mephibosheth onto theirs and began to ride up the hill, just above Saul's palace. Rizpah began to throw dirt in the air, crying out in grief and horror at what was happening. She threw her outer garment over her head and bowed low to the ground, her whole body writhing and groaning in agony.

As the horses galloped up the hill with the company of soldiers and her sons and the grandsons of Saul on their backs, Rizpah could see where they were headed. It was a small plateau at the top of the butte about a half-mile from Saul's palace, where everyone in the surrounding area could see. Just before reaching the top, she saw David's men hand the harness straps of the horses of those who had been incarcerated into the hands of the Gibeonite regiment. All but two of David's regiment then headed back toward Jerusalem, turning their backs on the Gibeonites and their captives as if they could not bear to watch what was about to happen while the others continued up the hill.

In the terror of the preceding moments, the palace maids and servants had scattered. They gathered up their belongings in a flurry and began to run down the hill toward the city. Rizpah momentarily let her eyes turn from the earth below her and from the horses in the distance and looked around only to realize that she was completely alone now.

How long had she been weeping? It seemed but a moment—and yet an eternity as well.

As she lifted her tear-stained face and puffy eyes toward the palace stalls and apartments, she could see that not only was there no Saul, no Ahinoam, no Abner or Phoebe—no one was in sight. She was truly and utterly alone. With the exception of a few chickens, not even a sound of animals left in the sheds could be heard. Everyone was gone. There was, in fact, no sound on the palace grounds except for her sniffles and the thud of her falling tears on the dirt beneath her. The servants had all run in terror, fearing for their lives as minions of Saul. She could not blame them—her sons were innocent of war crimes and the soldiers took them. Why would they spare the life of a servant? She understood and felt no animosity toward them. There was a day when she would have run as well, but not today.

Rizpah looked back toward the butte and immediately became engrossed in what her eyes beheld. Noticing that the soldiers had reached their supposed destination as they dismounted their horses, she observed something that she had not seen before. It was a team of horses near the rear of the regiment pulling a load of logs. What were those for? What was about to happen? She needed to get closer to see the horror that she feared was about to befall her sons and the grandsons of Saul. She ran to her palace apartment and without thinking threw some clothes into a bag and then ran to the cook's quarters and grabbed two leather pouches of water and some flatbread that somehow was left behind by those who had already scattered. They had gone in one direction down the hillside of Gibeah. Her destination was in the opposite direction, up the hillside. She refused to let fear overcome her.

Flinging the water pouches over one shoulder and the knotted bag of cloth and flatbread over the other, Rizpah began her half-mile trek up the hill with her eyes fixed on the men at the top of the hill. They did not notice her, but her eyes did not leave them. Some were digging holes in the ground, and some were unloading the logs from the horses. They were laying them on the ground and tying them in some fashion. She could not know what they were doing for sure, but assumptions began to race through her mind.

Others were pulling her sons and the five grandsons of Saul from the backs of the horses and throwing them to the ground. They then proceeded to kick and whip and bludgeon the young men. Rizpah could hardly bear it. Her heart was pounding so strongly that she thought it might explode within her. Grief and determination carried her up the hill.

In minutes, she was within two stones throw from the men and could hear them cursing at Armoni and Mephibosheth and the five grandsons of Saul. She began to sob. She threw down her natural burdens and ran toward her spiritual ones. She ran toward Armoni and laid herself across him to spare him the blow of the Gibeonites' whips. It ripped into her flesh, and the soldier grabbed her by the hair and tossed her aside like an empty sack. She landed on a boulder, hitting her head, and fell back on the face of the rock. Then she felt the boot of the menacing soldier in her abdomen and his spit running down the back of her neck. As she attempted to get up, everything was spinning around her. She could hear the cries of her sons and the mocking tones of the soldiers, but could not decipher clearly what they were saying. They were fading from view…then everything went black.

As she awakened and leaned forward to try to get up, she immediately felt the sting of the open flesh on her back and the bruised or broken ribs she had incurred at the boot of the soldier. Everything was blurry, but not spinning anymore; she could barely move. She could not hear the voices of the abusing soldiers any longer or smell the stench of the horses on which they rode. It seemed to be early morning and not late afternoon any longer—how long she had been out was unclear. What she did know was that every movement she made was a motion in pain.

Where were the soldiers, where were her sons? It seemed to take Rizpah an eternity just to lift her head, much less her body. With two knees on the ground and one hand resting on the large flat rock beneath her, she brushed the hair back from her face and slowly looked up. To her utter horror, her dear, precious Armoni and Mephibosheth and the five grandsons of Saul were bloody, bruised, and beaten to death and left hanging on crosses.

The abusing soldiers were gone, with the exception of two of David's soldiers, who remained to guard "the sacrifice" until further notice. Only her two dear sons and the grandsons of Saul remained, hanging for everyone in the surrounding valley to see. She had no cutting instrument to cut them down, and she had no digging tool to bury them with. Even if she had, the soldiers would have prohibited her from doing so. Weeping filled her soul, and though her body was wracked with pain, it could not match the agony she felt in her heart. Life would never be the same.

What was it that old Phoebe had said? *"Days of darkness are upon you, but the light of Jehovah goes before you."* As the recent engravings of her heart began to surface, she could feel the Presence of Jehovah beginning to fill her with a sense of calm, a strange sense of peace. From the time Rizpah was a child, in some of her darkest moments, Phoebe had taught her that "weeping may endure for a night, but joy comes in the morning." [1] They had put the words to melody and sung the tune over and over on many cloud-filled days until her young faith was renewed. Now, in her darkest hour, that melody permeated Rizpah's being and strangely renewed her hope in an old familiar way. Yes, "days of darkness" were definitely upon her, but surely "the light of Jehovah" had come up to this mountain before her! What mixed emotions, what strange companions grief and faith were, but what hope they left her with on this rock. She knelt on the rock, lifting her hands toward heaven, her tears of grief and faith blending together as they streamed down her cheeks. She offered a confession of trust to the all-wise One.

Rizpah looked again upon the bodies of her sons and realized that not only were they exposed to the eyes of the two remaining soldiers and the elements of the air, but they were also exposed to the Lord God Jehovah. The sacrifice of their lives was not in vain; it was clearly before the Lord. Her dear, precious sons were *before the Lord.…*

Rizpah whispered, "I will lift up my eyes to the hills—from where does my help come? My help comes from the Lord, who made heaven and earth. He will not allow my foot to be moved; He who keeps me will not slumber nor sleep. The Lord is my keeper; He is my shade at my right hand. The sun shall not strike me by day, nor the moon by night. The Lord will preserve me from all evil; He shall preserve my soul. The Lord will preserve me from this time forth and forevermore." [2]

There would come a day in the future when another woman would stand by her son as he too hung on a cross before the Lord. She was another mother who would grieve with eyes of faith. That woman was Mary, the mother of Jesus. Every mother sees the future in the eyes of her children just as Rizpah did. It's likely, as well, that the widowed Mary looked to her firstborn son, Jesus, to provide for her naturally before she fully realized that His spiritual provision would supersede anything natural that He might offer her in the years ahead, although He took care of the natural as well when He commissioned his disciple John to take care of His mother at the cross. I'm sure that as Mary stood at the foot of the cross, she too had a blending of tears of grief and faith—the grief of a mother and the faith of a daughter of God. The fact is that as much as we see the future in the eyes of our children, the future rests securely only in the eyes of God.

Initial shock and emotions of despair must have filled the hearts of both of these mothers. The horror of seeing their beloved sons on crosses must have pierced through every fiber of their beings. They must have looked on their sacrifice with redemptive despair—that is, despair that draws from God a peace that surpasses all natural understanding. It is despair that reflects utter dependence on the living God and draws on His grace. There is an ungodly despair as well, one that curses God and walks out on life emotionally, perhaps physically, one that dwells in the cesspool of depression and anger, detesting all that life has to offer. Redemptive despair is beneficial to the soul; ungodly despair is not. Both are desperate and broken to the core, but one evokes healing and hope, while the other emits hopelessness and sickness of heart and body.

Ungodly despair is a flight from desire; it is a refusal to embrace loss… [It] refuses to dream, to hope, and to move with courage toward what we will one day become.… Godly despair is the collapse of self-will; it is the surrender to a reality of becoming.… Instead of a suicide note that puts a stop to the loss, it is a howling prayer that sees no explanation for our pain but reflexively knows something beyond an answer is what we desire. Although ungodly despair demands an answer for the loss, it would refuse to accept an answer even if it were hand-delivered by God. Godly despair cries out for perspective but allows the hollowness of loss to move the heart to seek God.[3]

Grief and despair have many faces, many moods. Faith has one face, one that looks up to the One on Whom it can depend. It cries out to an all-knowing God, but it does not demand an explanation of the now, knowing that it will be lovingly and mysteriously carried through to the tomorrow. This faith not only understands, but also embraces the fact that life is challenging and difficult. In that knowledge alone is hope and victory. "Once we truly know that life is difficult—once we truly understand and accept it—then life is no longer difficult. Because once it has been accepted, the fact that life is difficult no longer matters."[4]

✦ Most of the Psalms were composed in the midst of David's darkest trials. Most of the Epistles were written from prisons. The deep emotions of loss are not limited to family deaths. When Rizpah's sons died she not only lost them; she lost her world as she knew it—life changed for her forever. Loss of a job, loss of a spouse due to divorce, loss of retirement monies, loss of a home, loss of health, a barren womb, a kidnapped child, or birth of a handicapped child can all have the effects of shock

and despair. "We usually don't ask for brokenness or barrenness, but God in His infinite wisdom sees to it that we go
through what is necessary." [5]

✦   Many people throughout history have made their greatest mark
    on history in their darkest trials: Lincoln during the Civil War,
    Churchill during World War II, Florence Nightingale in her
    bedridden illness, Corrie ten Boom in her prison camp, William
    and Catherine Booth in their poverty, Joni Eareckson Tada in
    her quadriplegia. The difference between these historic heroes
    of faith and those who dwell in a pool of pity is that these
    people embraced the trial and demanded that the test become
    a testimony. "Sometimes it seems that when God is about to
    make preeminent use of a man, he puts him through the fire." [6]
    In embracing the fiery trial, the dross rises to the top and
    the gold is purified. It's then that destiny is on the verge of
    being realized.

Many people live as though they regret God's incredible invitation to life. Avoiding pain becomes their chief occupation. And
few of them realize that avoidance of difficulty only produces
more pain in the long run.... The Bible, above all else, seems to be
a book of reality. And reality has the mark of difficulty. On one
side is the message of hope. The Scriptures say that the righteous
shall flourish like the palm tree—but we need to remember that
palm trees don't grow in beautiful forests, but in the desert. We
are called to bear fruit—but we must recognize that the fruit tree
grows in valleys, not on mountaintops... I believe that pain and
suffering can either be a prison or a prism. The tests of life are not
to break us but to make us. [7]

In the midst of our greatest trials, it is our privilege and God's pleasure
that we would hold onto Him in faith, believing that He knows and sees
and will reward. He created us because He loves us, not to destroy us. Oh

yes, He desires to draw out of us all that distracts our mind and weakens our will, all that undermines our faith in Him. Yes, He will use whatever means necessary to grow our faith and to mold us into His Image, but He will not allow life to crush us to the point of utmost despair, nor will He leave us to bear the burden alone.

Paul writes in 2 Corinthians 4:8–14, 16–18:

We've been surrounded and battered by troubles, but we're not demoralized; we're not sure what to do, but we know that God knows what to do; we've been spiritually terrorized but God hasn't left our side; we've been thrown down, but we haven't broken. What they did to Jesus, they do to us—trial and torture, mockery and murder; what Jesus did among them, he does in us—he lives! Our lives are at constant risk for Jesus' sake, which makes Jesus' life all the more evident in us....

So we're not giving up. How could we! Even though on the outside it often looks like things are falling apart on us, on the inside, where God is making new life, not a day goes by without his unfolding grace. These hard times are small potatoes compared to the coming good times, the lavish celebration prepared for us. There's far more here than meets the eye. The things we see now are here today, gone tomorrow. But the things we can't see now will last forever. (The Message)

Grief and faith do seem to be strange companions, especially to those who do not know Christ. How can one grieve and have faith at the same time? This is a great mystery to the soul that is downcast and broken-hearted. To have faith seems contradictory to the power of grief, and yet it is not. However, not to have faith for the future, not to embrace the life a loved one would want you to live if he or she were still alive, is contradictory to the foundation stone of pure grief. Grief that is pure comes from a heart of love. It is love for the deceased that motivates one to live and not die with the deceased, or respect for the loss that stirs the heart to not give up on life. Grief that is selfish comes from a heart that has loved for a variety of reasons attached to self. Reasons such as an identity attachment, an overly dependent emotional attachment, or having lived vicariously through that person can all hinder a person from stepping into a life of faith and joyful expectation rather than dread.

Grieving over loss is not wrong; it is needed in fact. Grief can cleanse the soul of wounds and misperceptions. Grief's time should never be measured or compared. Crisis is unique to the individual and to the situation.

Every person's response to a crisis is unique. One's personal history, personality and even placement in the family can affect his or her response. The response is also dependent upon a variety of elements within the crisis itself:

✦ **Obstacles that appear to be overwhelming:** The obstacle could be a problem that would not be serious to most people, but for this individual has special significance. Examples of this might be the loss of a job, a sudden geographical move, or the loss of a pet.

✦ **Obstacles that appear to be cyclical or unending:** Sometimes a person may cope well with short-term problems, but not with long-term situations. Some examples of this would be hormonal problems, long-term debilitating illness, or marital separation.

✦ **Problems that occur at a vulnerable time:** Sometimes the main problem is usually cloaked in a series of minor crises. A problem that a person could normally cope with follows, and he or she loses control because normal coping mechanisms are not functioning at peak level.

✦ **Sudden shock:** Examples of this could be the sudden death of a loved one, the loss of a home due to fire or flooding, or the unanticipated birth of a handicapped child.

✦ **Giving birth, having surgery, or having medical tests:** These situations could be considered elements of a crisis in that they are a shock to the physical body and, in turn, affect the whole person.

✦   **The death of a loved one:** Every individual's grief will be unique depending on the type of death, the type of person, and the placement of the person in the family. The timing of the incident and the nature of the relationship with the deceased may also affect the response. Was the relationship a positive one or a negative one? Was it volatile or peaceful? These may be questions that you would want to seek out.[8]

All of these crises have elements within them that contain aspects of loss, evoking grief and the need for faith. Although grief is unique to the individual and to the situation, one common denominator often accompanies it—fear. Fear of the present, fear of the future, fear of what is and what isn't all must be faced squarely. The opposite of fear is faith: "Fear is self centered; faith is God centered."[9] Faith depends on God for its sustenance. Fear depends on a fragile self, knowing that it cannot stand much longer. "Fear tries to hold your world together; faith holds you together."[10] In the midst of loss, we must let go of the sorrow and fear that all-too-quickly becomes familiar and cling to faith.

Faith requires sacrifice, for it is sacrifice that demands courage, and courage develops the muscles of faith. A sacrifice that demands courage is almost always required when it comes to investing in the future in any degree. Whether it's normal daily living to be sacrificed for health issues, money to be sacrificed for an education, independence to be sacrificed for marital commitment and parenthood, or whatever the sacrifice may be, that's when fear loves to come walking through the door. Fear almost always announces the known costs and the unknown costs without announcing the benefits and blessings that God holds in store for your sacrifice. "Without the eyes of faith the soul is blind."[11] When faith is lacking, one of two things usually occurs: Either Satan creates imaginary reasons to fear, or the lack of faith enables natural circumstances to be magnified and spiritual realities to remain unseen. The soul needs eyes of faith just to meander through this time zone much less see into the next one.

To face the reality of daily living and life-challenging events, one must be willing to honestly face the facts, grieving the loss and walking in faith. To grieve without the intermingling of faith leaves one destitute of hope and a reason to go on living. On September 14, 2001, at the National Day of Prayer and Mourning, President George Bush said, "We learn in tragedy that His purposes are not always our own, yet the prayers of private suffering...are known and heard and understood." We must always remember that God is with us and that He hears our prayers. He is the One who will enable us to continue to put one foot in front of the other and to live another day. Yes, *live*—not in hopeless sorrow that is full of doubt and fear of what tomorrow may bring, but in expectant faith.

Grief and faith are indeed strange companions; yet one cannot exist without the other for many days, for faith comforts grief and grief matures faith. The two together are the sacrificed required. So go on living, knowing that you have permission to grieve when it hurts, to ask questions when you're perplexed, and to rejoice when all is well and when it is not. For joy does not come from everything being perfectly well, it comes from a complete trust in the One who "has made everything beautiful in its time..." [12]

A Posture of Peace, A Position of Faith

ISAIAH 26:3: *"You will keep him in perfect peace, whose mind is stayed on You, because he trusts in You."*

ISAIAH 26:12: *"LORD, You will establish peace for us, for You have also done all our works in us."*

ISAIAH 32:17-18: *"The work of righteousness will be peace, and the effect of righteousness, quietness and assurance forever. My people will dwell in a peaceful habitation, in secure dwellings, and in quiet resting place."*

ISAIAH 48:18-19: *"Oh, that you had heeded My commandments! Then your peace would have been like a river, and your righteousness like the waves of the sea. Your descendants also would have been like the sand, and the offspring of your body like the grains of sand; his name would not have been cut off nor destroyed from before Me."*

ISAIAH 52:7: *"How beautiful upon the mountains are the feet of him who brings good news, who proclaims peace, who brings glad tiding of good things, who proclaims salvation, who says to Zion, 'Your God reigns!'"*

ISAIAH 55:12: *"For you shall go out with joy, and be led out with peace; the mountains and the hills shall break forth into singing before you, and all the trees of the field shall clap their hands."*

ISAIAH 66:12-13: *"For thus says the LORD: 'Behold, I will extend peace to her like a river, and the glory of the Gentiles like a flowing stream. Then you shall feed; on her sides shall you be carried, and be dandled on her knees. As one whom his mother comforts, so I will comfort you; and you shall be comforted in Jerusalem.'"*

PROVERBS 12:20: *"Deceit is in the heart of those who devise evil, but counselors of peace have joy."*

PROVERBS 16:7: *"When a man's ways please the LORD, He makes even his enemies to be at peace with him."*

PSALM 4:8: *"I will both lie down in peace, and sleep; for You alone, O LORD, make me dwell in safety."*

PSALM 29:11: *"The LORD will give strength to His people; the LORD will bless His people with peace."*

PSALM 34:14: *"Depart from evil and do good; seek peace and pursue it."*

PSALM 37:11: *"But the meek shall inherit the earth, and shall delight themselves in the abundance of peace."*

PSALM 37:37: *"Mark the blameless man, and observe the upright; for the future of that man is peace."*

PSALM 55:18: *"He has redeemed my soul in peace from the battle that was against me."*

PSALM 119:165: *"Great peace have those who love Your law, and nothing causes them to stumble."*

NOTES

1   "For His anger is but for a moment, His favor is for life; *weeping* may endure for a night, but joy comes in the morning." (Psalm 30:5)

2   Paraphrase of Psalm 121.

3   Dr. Dan B. Allender and Dr. Tremper Longman III, *The Cry of the Soul: How Our Emotions Reveal Our Deepest Questions about God* (Colorado Springs, CO: NavPress, 1994), 147–8.

4   Scott Peck, *The Road Less Traveled* (New York: Simon & Schuster, 1978), 15.

5   Frank Damazio, *From Barrenness to Fruitfulness* (Ventura, CA: Regal Books, 1998), 39.

6   Tim Hansel, *You Gotta Keep Dancin'* (Colorado Springs, CO: Victor Cook Communications, 1985), 87.

7   Ibid., 87–8.

8   Glenda Malmin, *Woman You Are Called and Anointed* (Portland, OR: City Bible Publishing, 1998), 135–6.

9   Evangelist W. V. Grant, *Nuggets in a Nutshell* (Dallas, TX: Grant's Faith Clinic), #60, p. 3.

10   Ibid., #61, p. 3.

11   Ibid., #372, p. 16.

12   Ecclesiastes 3:11.

"Preying" at the Cross: Faith's Assailants

Watching While Waiting and Waiting While Watching

So they fell, all seven together, and were put to death in the days of harvest, in the first days in the beginning of barley harvest. Now Rizpah the daughter of Aiah took sackcloth and spread it for herself on the rock, from the beginning of harvest until the late rains poured on them from heaven. And she did not allow the birds of the air to rest on them by day nor the beasts of the field by night. — 2 Samuel 21:9b–10

Her hair was matted from the mixture of summer perspiration and the dust that she had flung into the open air over her head in grief. Dirt filled the dried cracks in Rizpah's hands and was imbedded under her nails as well. Her body reeked of a foul, pungent odor from a lack of bathing. She actually could not smell her own body odor any longer, but from the looks of the two guards who kept their distance from her and by her remembrance of the streets of her childhood, she knew it was there. Her clothing, which had been midnight blue and pewter gray in the beginning, was definitely the appropriate black for mourning now. It had been six long months and parasitic lice bored their way into her scalp, making her vigil all the more miserable. She had known poverty before; she had smelled it, walked in it, and tasted it, but never like this. There were no passersby on this hillside to offer her a new scarf or a bit of soap, but neither were they there to mock her or offer her their pseudo-pity either. On most days the tormentor of her soul would have her believe that she was, as her father had told her over and over again, just "a bit of worthless pavement."

In the first two months, along with her mourning garments, Rizpah had also worn a cloth over her mouth and nose to help prevent the nauseating stench of the rotting bodies of her sons and the grandsons of Saul from causing her to gag. Though she had little to eat, hardly a day went by that she did not spew vomit from the rancid smell of decomposition.[1] Even though the only food she ate was bits of leftover flatbread that the guards tossed aside out of pity for her, it had still come up easily when the sun was too hot and the smell of the decomposing bodies rose with the temperatures.

When Rizpah frantically left the palace grounds so many months ago to follow her sons and the soldiers up the hill, she had quickly tossed some things in a bag not really realizing what they were. Much to her surprise, she had scooped into the bag a sheet of black sackcloth that was used for mourning. It was the same one she had used for mourning when the news of Saul's death had come to her years before. Without knowing it, she had also tossed one of her firstborn's swaddling bands into the bag. She wept both in grief and in joy when she first saw the swaddling band. Such sweet memories flooded her soul, and yet the sorrow of the loss overwhelmed her. It was almost as if Jehovah had put that swaddling band in her bag to offer her comfort and memories of His blessings in her life.

During the initial two months of her intercessory vigil on the rock, the swaddling band of her precious firstborn babe was worn to cover her face from the stench of his rotting body. The memory of his sweet babyhood was dear, but the existence of his decaying body was her current reality.

After the first terrifying day and night, Rizpah spread out her mourning cloth on the rock she had been brutally thrown against, and it became her rock of intercession. The cloth was made of black goat hair. It was coarse and rough, but it provided a covering for her from the blistering sun in the summer, and now, in these last two months of the cold night breezes of fall, it was thick enough to keep her warm.[2] When this all began, due to the drought conditions, the weather was already hot even though it was only late spring. Then she went through the even more agonizing temperatures of summer. It had been blistering hot for four months; but now, though it was seasonably warm for fall during the day, it was cold at night. The emptiness of her stomach and the temperatures made her shiver at night, but the awareness of Jehovah's Presence gave her a warmth that words could not explain and the body could not fully absorb.

Everything about the horror of the seven crosses assaulted the senses. The smell in the first six weeks or so had been putrefying; it was an odor that could not be removed in the warm breezes of late spring or the baking sun of summer. No matter how open the air was, this smell over-powered any she had ever experienced in any childhood slum. In the initial weeks, while the intestines and what remained in them were rotting, the bodies were bloated and nauseating to the senses.[3] The odor was permeating; it saturated the air, Rizpah, and likely the two guards standing at a distance as well. It was a stench that not only permeated clothing and the very pores of the skin, but also engraved its memory on the walls of the mind. Just momentarily reflecting back on that odor could almost make her retch.

However, in the last four months something had changed. Though the bodies were still clearly decomposing, the odor of death had altered from something foul and rancid to an indescribable faint sweet fragrance. It was confusing to the senses and would have been difficult to describe to anyone. It was like the fragrance of delicate pastry bread; it was some-thing like a fragrance she remembered smelling from the cook's kitchen when Saul had special houseguests.[4] It was as though a sweet fragrance of sacrifice was being offered up to the Lord.

Though the odor of the sacrificed bodies had mysteriously changed, the sight of the disintegration process had not become less repulsive.

After the food and intestines had decomposed, the dehydration of the bodies began and the bloating disappeared slowly. Since muscles decompose more slowly, the bodies remained in virtually the same locked position as when they were first hung on the crosses. Under the baking sun of summer, the slow dehydration caused the decomposing bodies to become nothing but leathery skin stretched tightly over bones.[5] Rizpah thought they might fall from their cross of death into her loving arms, but because there was little flesh to begin with around the wrists and ankles, the ropes were still taut. She watched her beautiful sons literally become skin and bones before her very eyes. It was a slow degeneration that was horrifying for anyone to behold with the natural eye, much more so for a mother.

Then there were the vultures.... The aggression of the giant birds required her to be on a constant watch. They were greedy and unscrupulous predators on a normal day, but in this drought they were more than determined to take advantage of their find. She watched in utter horror on the first morning as one of the vultures came and plucked out the eye of one of the grandsons of Saul and then began to peck at his head. She broke a brittle branch from the nearby mulberry tree and ran toward the cross screaming at the vulture, "Away! Away! Away, you vile creature!"

The two guards looked on from a distance with pity, but she cared little what they thought of her. From that day on she kept a close eye on the sky, ever watching the circling birds, protecting not only her sacrifice but also the sacrifice of Israel.

Then there were the starving jackals and wild dogs, known for biting at the deceased as they hung on crosses, tugging at them continually in an attempt to pull them down and devour them. She could see their beady eyes in the night and hear their piercing, barking howls. The "anwa" always began with a high-pitched, long, drawn-out cry. This repeated two or three times, each time in a higher key than before. Then finally there were several short, loud, yelping barks. As the pitch raised, others would join in.[6] The threatening anwa howl of these predators had never bothered her when she was safely in Saul's palace, but out here on the rock, it tormented and poked at her faith.[7] Their bony bodies were starving, and they were determined to have their fill. Out of mercy the two guards had allowed Rizpah a stick of burning wood from their fire so that she could build a small fire near her mourning cloth. If the skulking jackals came too close, she ran at them with a torch of fire and tormented them in return. In the early weeks, she had allowed herself little sleep in the day or the night for fear that these vile predators, these assailants of her faith, would devour her sacrifice.

Other than tossing some occasional leftover pieces of flatbread in her direction and allowing her to have a stick of burning wood from their fire, the guards never spoke to Rizpah or offered her help; they kept their distance. They were only there to make sure that no one came and stole the bodies or let them down until King David gave the orders to do so. So it was there on that rock that she kept a constant vigil, standing in solidarity with her nation—and yet alone.

The physical challenges Rizpah faced each day were certainly more than she had ever borne before, but they paled in comparison to the spiritual journey she had been on these past six months. When she and Armoni and Mephibosheth had first arrived home from old Phoebe's house, though in a state of alarm, the servants had clearly told her the rumors that in order to end the drought, Jehovah had directed king David to seek out the Gibeonites. Hastily they told her that as atonement for Saul's slaughtering of the Gibeonites, which was in direct disobedience to their treaty with Joshua four centuries ago, they requested seven of Saul's descendents to be hung on crosses to die—the perfect number of sacrifice. Before they could say anymore, the soldiers had arrived and taken Rizpah's sons along with Saul's five grandsons. So Rizpah knew that even though she was alone on the rock as a mother, she was standing in solidarity with her nation before a holy God.

Initially Rizpah could hardly bear the personal sacrifice, much less believe the requirement. She simply demanded of her body that it do what must be done to get up the hill. Then after being tossed aside so ruthlessly and knocked unconscious, she awakened the next morning confessing her trust in Jehovah, but then found herself weeping for days without ceasing. She wept until the circumstances finally demanded of her to flail her arms and scream at the top of her lungs to the taunting birds of the air and the beasts of the night. Then, still in disbelief at what was really happening, she imagined her sons stepping down from the crosses and coming back to life.

The cruelest of all predators came to her when she least expected it, when she would fall asleep. The faces of her maids and servants flashing through her mind, *"Come back to the palace dear Rizpah. They're dead. Don't you see? They're dead."* Her father's voice would thunder to her, *"You foolish woman. Get off that rock and do something with your life. You'll never amount to anything in life watching the dead!"* The faces of Ahinoam's sons would startle her dreams as well with accusatory tones: *"Who do you think you are? What are you trying to prove? No royal blood flows in your veins; it's time you left this mountain!"* Night after night, Rizpah was tormented by dreams that invaded her sleep, only to startle awake to lurking green eyes in the darkness that required of her yet one more fiery charge.

In the following days, questions began to ricochet off the walls of her mind. She began to bargain with Jehovah. *"If You will but do this miracle for me, I will offer myself on the altar of sacrifice to the Gibeonites. I am but a mere woman in this world, but I am Your daughter. Release this miracle for me, my dear Jehovah. I know that it is within Your reach. Breathe life into my sons once again, and I will serve You in any way that You desire for all the days of my life. Please, Jehovah, have mercy upon my dear sons."*

When the days of silence engulfed her and the stench of the rotting and bloated bodies sent nauseating waves through the very fiber of her soul, she became enraged with Jehovah. Angry accusations spewed from her mouth toward heaven: "You do not see! If You do, You certainly do not care. Which is worse, oh my soul, that my God does not see or that He does not care? I hate You! I hate what You have allowed and I hate You! Have I not had enough suffering in my life; am I Your pawn in this cruel game of life? My seed was my only hope in this world of cruel disappointment, my only light in this tunnel of constant despair. Why have You taken my dear sons from me? Armoni was to be grand, elevated to high position, and Mephibosheth studied Your Law and was anxious to expose the shame of Baal. You gave them to me as gifts; they were destined to serve You. They wanted to make a difference in this life, to reach further and to do more than their egocentric father had ever done. Why them? Why do You require their blood, was not Saul's enough? Why? Why!"

After days of anger, sadness encompassed her. It had been three very long weeks, and the anger that had turned to rage and then to self-depre-cation had subsided, but sorrow now filled her soul and ran over onto her mourning cloth. No more dirt was thrown in the air in grief; there was no more tearing at her hair, pulling out her eyelashes, or biting her nails. Only overwhelming sorrow remained in her soul. "*Where are You, Jehovah? Why are You hidden from me? My soul longs for You. Do You not see me? I am depleted of accusations and only long for Your Presence to return. Come to me, Jehovah. No longer leave me alone on this rock.*"

Rizpah could hardly lift her head or her body from the rock. She slept endlessly for days as a heavy veil of depression covered her, pushing her down until she felt as though she was becoming flattened into the mourning cloth. The only time she rose was if she heard a vulture in the sky mocking her or the anwa howl of the lurking jackals. Then she would jerk awake and chase them with her fiery poker and in a daze gather more sticks for the burning fire.

She was so deeply pressed by the heaviness of her soul that she felt almost as if she was becoming one with the darkness of the mourning cloth. Murky thoughts made their way through the fog in her mind: "*Was it the mourning cloth or the rock that she was becoming one with? No matter, she could not lift herself out of the darkness regardless of what she was glued to. The heaviness was simply too heavy.*" The sorrow pierced so deeply into her heart that even her muscle tissue and bones seemed to ache. Her entire being was wracked with pain, both emotionally and physically. The agony she felt penetrated more deeply than anything she ever could have imagined.

As the days and nights continued to pass, Rizpah's sorrow melted into tender humility and her humility into a prayer of surrender and desire for the Lover of her soul. In her waking moments, she groaned in the tenderness of her soul: Jehovah, You are my Rock; my soul loves You. Forgive me for my words of anger. You are my hope, my strong tower, and my shield. You alone are my comforter, the one in whom I trust. Yes, yes, my trust is in You and You alone. "Have mercy upon me, O God, according to Your lovingkindness; according to the multitude of Your tender mercies, blot out my transgressions. Wash me thoroughly from my iniquity, and cleanse me from my sin. Create in me a clean heart, O God, and renew a steadfast spirit within me. Do not cast me away from Your presence, and do not take Your Holy Spirit from me. Restore to me the joy of Your salvation, and uphold me by Your generous Spirit." [8]

The words of Phoebe began to surface in Rizpah's mind: *"Jehovah's ways are higher than your ways. You must not question, but rather stand strong, for Jehovah is with you and will be by your side. Though your sacrifice will be great, know that no sacrifice goes unnoticed by Jehovah, the Rock of your salvation. The Most High God goes before you and prepares the way. He will be with you and will watch over you. He will comfort you and hear your cry. He will answer your prayers and the prayers of generations to come...do not fear...Jehovah will be with you."*

As the words came pouring back into Rizpah's mind, the weight of depression lifted. The shock, the anger, and the heaviness were gone; they dissipated as she reached for and embraced the Word of God. Yes, Jehovah was with her. He was with her and with her sacrifice, the sacrifice of Israel. The seven bodies were still before her eyes, the assailants of her faith still screeched in the sky and lurked behind the trees nearby, but the eyes of her understanding were opened. She could feel faith welling up within her once again. Her sons' lives were not lost to the pool of insignificance, and neither was hers.

Sensing the closeness of Jehovah, she straightened herself and stood tall on the rock with her head held high. Although the vile predators of the sky and the land were starving from the long drought, they were forbidden to feast on Rizpah's sacrifice. No, they would not have any piece of the sacrifice of Israel on her watch. Her shouts transitioned from rebuking threats to the fowls of the air and the anwa of the jackals to praises to her God. She marched around the crosses and praised Jehovah for His ever-faithful Presence: "I praise You, Jehovah. Let Your Presence chase these predators from my sacrifice. You are my God, my Rock in whom I trust. You are the God of the heavens and the Watchman of the sky. I praise You! I praise You!"

Rizpah's shouts of praise were more resounding than her previous fear-filled threats, and the vultures looked on with almost humorous confusion and seeming frustration. Even the onlooking guards seemed confused by her determined step and shouts of victory. The jackals and wild dogs feared fire and she no longer feared anything, so these hideous predators were not a match for this fiery anointed woman of faith either. She was no mere piece of pavement; she was a hot fiery coal on the tip of an arrow, determined to hit the mark destined for her.

She no longer cared how hot it was in the blazing sun or how cold it got at night—Rizpah would not leave this rock until signs of blessing poured down from heaven and her sons' lives hit the mark that God destined for them. She would stand in solidarity with her sons, with her nation, and with her God and see destiny fulfilled. She would remain until the drought was dispelled and showers of blessing filled the earth.

Even though she was standing alone, seemingly hidden from the view of all that should be watching and waiting with her, she knew that she was not alone; the One True God was with her. She would continue her victorious vigil, watching over the sacrifice and waiting for God's redemptive sign that it had been found acceptable in His sight. The assailants of her faith no longer had sway over her.

Destiny was in the making, and her sons were going to be part of it one way or another. She would do her part and protect the sacrifice offered, and Jehovah would do His. She carried a fire within her spirit, as well as in her hands. So the waving of her stick of fire and her shouting march around the crosses became more than a warning to threatening predators; it became a march and a wave offering unto the Lord God, a sacrifice of praise for what He was about to do.

That faith had remained strong in her heart the last four months of this six-month vigil. Now when she chased and poked at a vulture or screamed at a band of jackals with a fiery stick in her hand, she did it with purpose and vision, with strength of mind and spirit. She and her sons might be hidden from the view of most, but her faith was undefeatable and her assailants would be vanquished and her sacrifice found acceptable in the eyes of the Lord. Her sons were dead, but they would not be forgotten. The pathway of their lives had gone in a direction other than her choosing, but their destinies would still be fulfilled. Their sacrifices would expose the shame of Baal by a nation being restored to blessing and fruitfulness. They would hit the mark of their callings and be elevated into the very presence of Jehovah. She would not leave this rock until rain fell from heaven validating her sacrifice.

Phoebe's words comforted her: *"Though your sacrifice will be great, know that no sacrifice goes unnoticed by Jehovah, the Rock of your salvation."* She realized now that those were not only the words of Phoebe, but the very words of God. Yes, the sacrifice of her sons was great, but they were indeed "before the Lord"; He had them in His eye-view from the moment of their capture. They were never really held by the ropes of their captors; they were embraced in the very arms of God. He had not left her alone on a rock; He was the Rock that had been with her all along. Had Jehovah not told her that He had gone before her preparing the way? Had he not told her that he would answer her prayers?

Lost in thought and meditation, Rizpah suddenly realized that her uplifted face and the top of her tunic were both wet with raindrops. The rains of refreshing were beginning to fall; in fact, they were beginning to pour.[9] Her sacrifice was accepted. As she stood in solidarity with her nation, the rains of blessing fell on her, on her sacrifice, and on the land. As she lifted her hands to feel the blessing of God, heaven's raindrops intermingled with her tears of thanksgiving.

Not only did Rizpah have to suffer the loss of her sons and the elements of the outdoor weather, but she also had to work hard to keep predators from disrespecting the value of the sacrificed bodies by preying on them and on her faith. We too must guard and protect that which the Lord has given to us to be a steward over. Why pray for an influential vocation only to come late, leave early, and pilfer the company's goods? Why attend college, sacrificing large sums of money and time, and not protect that sacrifice with study and prayer? Why pray that you might have a marriage and family, only to offer it up on the altar of materialism and career or self-promotion? Why ask the Lord for a ministry call, only to feast on carnality continually and not cultivate the garden of that calling with sincere humility and prayer and study of His Word?

Rizpah's example has much to teach us. Her task was not an easy one, her sacrifice was not small, and her grief was neither short nor simple. She didn't hide her heart in ongoing depression, resentment, or anger; she was busy in the midst of her grief. In the depth of her grief she stood in solidarity with her nation and protected that which the Lord had required of both her and her nation.

Rizpah's faith was undoubtedly altered during this six-month period. It must have grown and developed as it was challenged, harassed, and strengthened. She "watched while she waited" and "waited while she watched." She wept in the bitterness of her soul, groaned in agony, and cried out to a seemingly empty sky. Her patience must have been painfully exercised while waiting for God's affirmation and blessings. She encountered assailants to her faith and learned how to conquer them. One could surmise that she went into this experience weaker in faith than how she came out. Rizpah grieved before the crosses of death and the decomposition of her sons. This was a hard place—in the natural it was nothing more than a rough grieving cloth on an impenetrable rock. It was not a place of comfort, and yet the Comforter would come. It was not a place of joy, but the rejoicing that had been placed within her heart so long ago would be unlocked once again. It was a place in which she stood in solidarity with the population of a nation and yet was alone. It was the residence of the preying assailants of her faith and a place of waiting. It was a place where God was hidden from her view and a place where the innocent suffered.

Why do the innocent suffer? Have you ever asked that question? Some ask it boldly, others are afraid to ask, but all want to know the answer. Most know that the answer can only truly be found in the Answerer. However, the suffering of the innocent is certainly a mystery to us all, especially when it camps at our own personal doorstep. To say anything less than that is reductionistic in thinking and indicative of intellectual and spiritual arrogance.

The topic of suffering is not merely an intellectual issue to be debated among philosophers and academic theologians. It is an intensely personal issue to the believer in Christ and is likely the single biggest obstacle in the pathway of honest seekers of faith. When it is debated carelessly by thoughtless intellectuals, or invades someone's life that is close to us, it can tie our faith into emotional knots and leave us wandering aimlessly with spiritual vertigo. It can be disorienting, frustrating, and even paralyzing to one's faith.

We must remember, though, that "However, only in a world where faith is difficult can faith exist." [10] Without downs there are no ups; without valleys there are no mountains, without sorrow there is no joy, without challenges there is no reason for faith. Faith means believing in advance what will only make sense in retrospect. Even then, it may only be seen when one crosses over into eternity.

We must get over the idea that life is fair. The agony that the sinless Christ suffered on the cross demolished that concept once and for all.:

Jesus offered no immunity, no way out of the unfairness, but rather a way through it to the other side.... The primal desire for

fairness dies hard, and it should. Who among us does not sometimes yearn for more justice in this world here and now? Secretly,
I admit, I yearn for a world "fault-proof" against disappointment.... But if I stake my faith on such a fault-proof earth, my
faith will let me down. Even the greatest of miracles do not
resolve the problems of this earth: all people who find physical
healing eventually die. We need more than miracles. We need a
new heaven and a new earth, and until we have those, unfairness
will not disappear.[11]

Faith is not the ability to endure unfairness or hardship with a smile;
it is not even merely the ability to somehow see beyond it. There's more to
it than that. It all begins with a person—the Person. Jesus is the Answer to
the question of suffering and faith. Faith is birthed in a trusting relationship with Him; it comes to light in His Presence. In human relationships,
friends and lovers don't just want e-mails and phone calls—they want
presence. They want the other person to be with them. Solutions are not
always expected or needed, but *presence* is almost always desired. Jesus
longs for your presence, and you need His. It's Jesus who bears the
burden of pain and suffering with us; it's Him who makes the difference:

God's answer to the problem of suffering is that he came right
down into it.... If we want to be with God, we have to be with
suffering, we have to not avoid the cross, either in thought or in
fact. We must go where he is and the cross is one of the places
where he is. And when he sends us the sunrises, we thank him for
the sunrises; when he sends us sunsets and deaths and sufferings
and crosses, we thank him for that.... Even if I don't find myself
emotionally capable of doing that right now, even if I cannot
honestly say to God in the middle of pain, "God, thank you for
this pain," but have to say instead, "Deliver me from evil," that's
perfectly right and perfectly honest—yet I believe that's not the
last word. The last words of the Lord's prayer aren't "deliver us
from evil"; the last words are "Thine is the glory and the honor."[12]

Faith is not just the ability to bear contradiction and suffering, nor is it simply to be free of it either. Faith embraces suffering on the Rock of His Presence and turns it into glory. Romans 8:18 says, "For I consider that the sufferings of this present time are not worthy to be compared with the glory which shall be revealed in us." Faith like Rizpah's cannot be shaken because it is the very product of shaking. It cannot be dishonored because it receives glory and honor when that which is reproached is transformed into an acceptable sacrifice to the Lord. There is no lower depth that it can go and no higher place it can ascend to. Faith and glory are found in and on the Rock.

Our human nature yearns for a shortcut or even a longer, easier way around this pathway of suffering, but shortcuts and easier ways usually lead to stunted growth. Although pain is neither easy nor desirable, it is likely needed for a reason bigger than our minds can comprehend. Regardless of the reason, the outcome, or the length of time, faith becomes invincible when it is allowed to mature as it travels the pathway of grief. Growth takes place in the fertile valley of pain and suffering in a way that it could not on the more visible, easy-access plains of life.

Grief is never easy on the heart or the body. It is a lonely and difficult task that affects the spirit, soul, and body. It is, perhaps, the most misunderstood and neglected growth process a person's faith can go through. It's not that grief is a requirement of faith, but it is often needed in the development of faith. Grief is a normal, natural response to loss, and it takes courage and a strong belief system to ride the currents of turmoil and loss smoothly. Emotional responses in the midst of it all too often reveal what is happening in the vertical direction with God as well as the horizontal level with others. Grief reaches out for faith, then recoils, only to reach out again. Faith takes grief by the hand and simply holds on until the emotions of the heart are at peace.

All loss is significant—one person's loss is not more important than another's, and one person's grief should not be compared to another's. The grief process is unique to the individual and to the circumstance or lost relationship. It is meant to free us by leading us to a place of utter dependence on the Lord. It is a journey of faith. To see grief and faith in the same context seems contradictory, but in reality it is not. Both are honest expressions of the heart; both demand action. Grief leads one down the pathway of ultimate surrender and trust, and faith does as well. "Grief is a conflicting mass of human emotion that we experience following any major change in a familiar pattern of behavior." [13]

Graduating from high school and starting college, getting married, or changing vocations can create a sense of loss. Losing a home to fire or flooding, losing a spouse to death or divorce, the birth of a handicapped child, the loss of a body limb, or the loss of a friend or relative to drugs or alcoholism also evoke emotions of loss. All of these not only benefit from appropriate grief; they also reach for faith in the midst of the process in order to make sense of it all or simply to be motivated to continue on in life. Pain in life is inevitable, but camping out in the doldrums is definitely optional.

The typical "stages of grief as identified by Kubler-Ross in relation to death and dying" [14] relate to many kinds of grief:

The first stage is *denial*—not believing that it's really happening. The second stage is *bargaining*, trying to equivocate with God to make deals. The third stage is *anger*, the rage that comes from within based upon frustration which cannot be satiated. The fourth stage is *depression*, a symptom of both prolonged anger turned inward and guilt. The final stage is *acceptance*, realizing that what is, is—and is going to be. [15]

Whether or not a person goes through these exact stages or in this precise order is not really important. This is merely a studied observation made by Kubler-Ross about what is common to the human condition. The point here is that grief cannot be rushed, and it does seem to have definite phases.

Rizpah chose to make her encampment of grief on a rock. This is significant because a rock represents a place of strength and asylum. For example, Jesus Christ is our Rock. Many verses in the Psalms refer to the Lord as our Rock, our Fortress, our Strength, and the Rock of our Salvation. Even though Rizpah's rock was a place of mourning, it was also a place that must have strengthened her for the task, as it was a place of strength—an "immovable foundation."[16] This was a long, tedious, and yet courageous watch. She endured and suffered long until she was sure that her sacrifice and the sacrifice of the nation had been accepted.

There are numerous preying assailants of faith today, just as there were with Rizpah. She dealt with vultures, jackals, and wild dogs, along with a mother's grieving heart and the burden of a nation. The enemies of your faith are likely different than Rizpah's and yet very much related. These predators are not designed to merely stretch and grow faith; they are designed to destroy it if possible. They vary in shape, size, and context; here are just a few assailants of faith:

✦ **Condemnation says, "I am not worthy of a miracle."** Revelation 12:10–11 says, "Then I heard a loud voice saying in heaven, 'Now salvation, and strength and the kingdom of our God, and the power of His Christ have come, for *the accuser of our brethren*, who accused them before our God day and night *has been cast down.*' And they overcame him by the blood of the Lamb and by the word of their testimony, and they did not love their lives to the death."

✦ **Depression says, "I have no hope."** Proverbs 17:22 says, "A merry heart does good, like medicine, but *a broken spirit dries the bones.*" Psalm 42:5 says, "Why are you cast down, O my soul? And why are you disquieted within me? *Hope in God*, for I shall yet praise Him For the help of His countenance."

✦ **Bitterness says, "Vengeance is mine."** Ephesians 4:31 says, *"Let all bitterness*, wrath, anger, clamor, and evil speaking *be put away from you*, with all malice." Romans 12:19 says, "Beloved, *do not avenge yourselves*, but rather give place to wrath; for it is written, *'Vengeance is Mine, I will repay,' says the Lord.*"

✦ **Lack of Forgiveness says, "They don't deserve forgiveness."** Ephesians 4:32 says, "And be kind to one another, tenderhearted, *forgiving one another,* even as God in Christ forgave you." Matthew 6:14–15 says, "For if you forgive men their trespasses, your heavenly Father will also forgive you. But *if you do not forgive men their trespasses, neither will your Father forgive your trespasses."*

✦ **Doubt says, "But..."** Romans 14:23 says, "But he who doubts is condemned if he eats, because he does not eat from faith; for *whatever is not from faith is sin."*

✦ **"Not Asking" says, "He sees me where I'm at."** James 4:2 says, "...Yet *you do not have because you do not ask."*

✦ **"I don't have faith" mentality says, "It's easy for others; it's just not my gift."** Romans 12:3 says, "For I say, through the grace given to me, to everyone who is among you, not to think of himself more highly than he ought to think, but to think soberly, as *God has dealt to each one a measure of faith."* Mark 9:24 says, "Immediately the father of the child cried out and said with tears, *'Lord, I believe; help my unbelief!'"*

✦ **Self-pity says, "God doesn't like me."** Jeremiah 31:3 says, "The LORD has appeared of old to me, saying: 'Yes, *I have loved you with an everlasting love;* therefore with lovingkindness I have drawn you.'"

✦ **Fear says, "I'm afraid..."** Isaiah 43:1–3 says, *"Fear not,* for I have redeemed you; I have called you by your name; you are Mine. When you pass through the waters, I will be with you; and through the rivers, they shall not overflow you. When you walk through the fire, you shall not be burned, nor shall the flame scorch you. For I am the Lord your God. The Holy One of Israel, your Savior..." Psalm 34:18 says, "The LORD is near to those who have a broken heart, and saves such as have a contrite spirit."

✦ **Lack of surrender says, "I want to do it my way."** Romans 12:1 says, "I beseech you therefore, brethren, by the mercies of God, that you present your bodies a living sacrifice, holy, acceptable to God, which is your reasonable service."

✦ **Past disappointments say, "You can't trust God."** Psalm 37:40 says, "And the LORD shall help them and deliver them; He shall deliver them from the wicked, and save them, because they trust in Him." Psalm 33:18–22 says, "Behold, the eye of the LORD is on those who fear Him, on those who hope in His mercy, to deliver their soul from death, and to keep them alive in famine. Our soul waits for the LORD; He is our help and our shield. For our heart shall rejoice in Him, because we have trusted in His holy name. Let Your mercy, O LORD, be upon us, Just as we hope in You."

✦ **Self-reliance says, "I can provide for myself."** Ephesians 2:8–10 says, "For by grace you have been saved through faith, and that not of yourselves; it is the gift of God, not of works, lest anyone should boast. For we are His workmanship, created in Christ Jesus for good works, which God prepared beforehand that we should walk in them."

✦ **Other voices say, "Give up; Quit; You're crazy to continue this vigil of faith."** Psalm 34:17 says, "The righteous cry out, and the LORD hears, and delivers them out of all their troubles." Proverbs 3:5–6 says, "Trust in the LORD with all your heart, and lean not on your own understanding; in all your ways acknowledge Him, and He shall direct your paths."

✦ **Sin says, "There's no hope for you."** Mark 2:5, 11 says, "When Jesus saw their faith, He said to the paralytic, 'Son, your sins are forgiven you.… I say to you, arise, take up your bed, and go to your house.'"

✦ **Faith in other things says, "Christ has nothing real to offer."** Isaiah 53:5 says, "But He was wounded for our transgressions, He was bruised for our iniquities; the chastisement for our peace was upon Him, and by His stripes we are healed." First Peter 2:24 says, "…who Himself bore our sins in His own body on the tree, that we, having died to sins, might live for right-eousness—by whose stripes you were healed."

I'm sure you could name even more preying assailants of faith. If you are going to fulfill the destiny that God has planned for you, you must not only allow yourself the freedom to experience grief, but you must also confront the assailants of your faith along the way. Grief is healthy, but allowing the enemies of your soul to devour your faith is not. They are ruinous, vile predators to you and to the generation looking on. In the midst of grief, you must continually reach out to the Healer of your soul and let His Presence carry you with His faith. Yes, God was hidden from Rizpah's view, but always within her reach. He may be hidden from your view, but you are not out of His sight.

God is sovereign over everything that happens, even things that happen that are contrary to His moral will. Throughout human history, God has and is still allowing evil to occur. He doesn't want evil to occur; He doesn't make it happen; but neither does it happen outside of His sovereign control. Satan and everyone in his kingdom, is currently being allowed in varying degrees to be an expression of evil. This does not mean that God will not or cannot intervene and deal with evil. His judgment on evil is progressive and is leading up to the conclusion of human history on earth. However, since all evil has not yet been confined to the lake of fire,[17] we must live with the mystery of why God allows the innocent to suffer at the hands of the wicked.

God, by His great grace, grants us peace, protection, and prosperity both naturally and spiritually. However, He doesn't have a set formula in His Word that guarantees this. We should believe and pray for His covering and blessing. Jesus taught us to pray, "Deliver us from the evil one." [18] However, we err if we somehow believe that we have the right to require earthly blessings of Him. He is the creator; we are the created. We do not demand of God our desires to be free from pain and suffering as "rights" to be granted; we ask. We should hope for it, believe for it, pray for it; but not demand or "require" it. If we embrace the misconception that God owes us earthly blessings apart from His grace, then when pain and suffering come to our doorstep, our faith is shattered. When that occurs, we either end up bitter toward God or feel like we somehow need to forgive Him for not coming through on His promises, all the while knowing that His promises were misperceived by our own self-righteous expectations.

At the same time, we are left in the great chasm of self-centered forgetfulness of Who is the Redeemer and who is the redeemed. It is Him who created us, paid a price for us, and truly loves and blesses us on a daily basis. He does so with an incredible everlasting love, care, and concern, with very little thanks in return. God's blessings come by way of His grace, not our fiery demands. We must never forget who is the creator and who is the created when we bring our petitions before the Lord. To do so is arrogant and ungrateful.

Our sin nature as well as our Western cultural thought patterns have persuaded us in recent generations to change privileges into so-called rights. Most cultures grow up believing that "Life is tough and then you die." We have grown up in a generation that believes no longer in the "pursuit of happiness," but rather the "right of happiness." We have slipped far from truly thankful hearts for the privileges of freedom that many paid for with their blood. Sadly, we have also been so consumed with petitioning God for our needs that we have neglected to ask Him what He might like us to do, or simply voice our thankfulness to Him for His daily blessings. He delights to answer our petitions. Psalm 84:11 says, "For the LORD God is a sun and shield; the LORD will give grace and glory; no good thing will He withhold from those who walk uprightly." But He also appreciates gratefulness.

If you have faith when you present your request before God to believe that "no good thing will He withhold," you must believe that the answer to your petition is on the way.

Just because you don't see it with your eyes is no proof it is not coming, for God said blessed is he that believeth for he shall see. Faith is no more faith after you see what faith reaches out for. The minute you see it, it changes from faith to sight. [19]

As long as Rizpah waited on the rock, she was in a posture of faith. As long as you wait on the Rock, you are in a posture of faith. As soon as the answer comes, faith rejoices because it sees and then awaits the next challenge. Just as muscles yearn for exercise so they will be strengthened and not atrophy, faith yearns for challenges so that it may grow. When the solutions to your challenges are seen and realized, faith stretches for more. To tell your faith muscles to quiet themselves is to tell them to atrophy.

Every good exercise enthusiast knows that it is healthy to rest your muscles after an extended series of exercising because this also brings refreshing and growth to the muscles. But after an appropriate exercise siesta, your muscles hunger for more challenge, yearning to see resulting growth. So do not become disheartened when rains of refreshing begin to fall and in the midst of enjoying the moment you see another challenge on the horizon.

You were made for challenge. God loves challenge, and you are created in His image. Rizpah's challenge to watch over her sons and the five grandsons of Saul lasted approximately six months. She was a devoted mother and member of society who would not give up her watch until the sacrifice had been obviously accepted. She would not quit her vigil until the Lord had acknowledged the sacrifice with clarity. Regardless of how many predators she had to deal with, she remained on the rock. How long or how many dissenting voices does it take for you to give up on that which the Lord has given to you to be a steward of? Do you leave your post the first time a difficulty comes your way? Are the voices of others louder and more influential in your thoughts than the voice of the Lord? How long is too long to wait on God? How much is too much when it comes to taking a stand?

Rizpah waited actively until the rains of blessing fell. You too will have seasons of waiting, of guarding, and of grieving. Some of the assailants of your faith will look much the same as the last ones you saw and heard, while others will have new faces, but know that they all can be vanquished on the Rock. When in doubt, remain on the Rock of your Salvation, and hold fast to your faith until the rains of refreshing fall on your sacrifice. Like Rizpah, you too should rejoice when the rains fall and your sacrifice has been received. It's when the obvious blessings of God come that you know you have received great grace and are now enabled to go on in life with stronger faith, holding your head up with dignity and yet in humility before a gracious God.

The Rock of Faith

From the Psalms

PSALM 18:2: *"The LORD is my rock and my fortress and my deliverer; my God, my strength, in whom I will trust; my shield and the horn of my salvation, my stronghold."*

PSALM 18:31: *"For who is God, except the LORD? And who is a rock, except our God?"*

PSALM 18:46: *"The LORD lives! Blessed be my Rock! Let the God of my salvation be exalted."*

PSALM 27:5: *"For in the time of trouble he shall hide me in His pavilion; in the secret place of His tabernacle he shall hide me; he shall set me high upon a rock."*

PSALM 28:1: *"To You I will cry, O LORD my Rock: do not be silent to me, lest, if You are silent to me, I become like those who go down to the pit."*

PSALM 31:2: *"Bow down Your ear to me, deliver me speedily; be my rock of refuge, a fortress of defense to save me."*

PSALM 31:3: *"For You are my rock and my fortress; therefore, for Your name's sake, lead me and guide me."*

PSALM 40:2: *"He also brought me up out of a horrible pit, out of the miry clay, and set my feet upon a rock, and established my steps."*

PSALM 61:2: *"From the end of the earth I will cry to You, when my heart is overwhelmed; lead me to the rock that is higher than I."*

PSALM 62:2: *"He only is my rock and my salvation; he is my defense; I shall not be greatly moved."*

PSALM 62:6: *"He only is my rock and my salvation; he is my defense; I shall not be moved."*

PSALM 62:7: *"In God is my salvation and my glory; the rock of my strength, and my refuge, is in God."*

PSALM 71:3: *"Be my strong refuge, to which I may resort continually; you have given the commandment to save me, for You are my rock and my fortress."*

PSALM 89:26: *"He shall cry to Me, 'You are my Father, my God, and the rock of my salvation.'"*

PSALM 92:15: *"To declare that the LORD is upright; He is my rock, and there is no unrighteousness in Him."*

PSALM 95:1: *"Oh come, let us sing to the LORD! Let us shout joyfully to the Rock of our salvation."*

NOTES

1   "Decomposition begins at the moment of death. At this stage it is caused by two factors: autolysis, the breaking down of tissues by the body's own internal chemicals and enzymes; and putrefaction, the breakdown of tissues by bacteria. These processes release gases that are the chief source of the characteristic odour of dead bodies." "Decomposition" From *Wikipedia, the Free Encyclopedia*, http://en.wikipedia.org/wiki/Decomposition.

2   "Sackcloth. Cloth made of black Goats' hair, coarse, rough, and thick, used for sacks, and also worn by mourners (Gen. 37:34; Gen. 42:25; 2 Sa 3:31; Est 4;1; Est 4:2; Psa 30:11, etc.), and as a sign of repentance." (Mat 11:21); Easton; *Bible Works*.

3   "Stage 3: Putrefaction—4 to 10 days after death; State of decay: *Bacteria break down tissues and cells, releasing fluids into body cavities. They often respire in the absence of oxygen (anaerobically) and produce various gases including hydrogen sulphide, methane, cadaverine and putrescine as by-products. People might find these gases foul smelling, but they are very attractive to a variety of insects. The build up of gas resulting from the intense activity of the multiplying bacteria, creates pressure within the body. This pressure inflates the body and forces fluids out of cells and blood vessels and into the body cavity.*" "Stages of Decomposition," *Decomposition: What Happens to the Body after Death?*
http://www.deathonline.net/decomposition/decomposition/putrefaction.htm.

4   "Stage 5: Butyric fermentation—20 to 50 days after death; State of decay: *All the remaining flesh is removed over this period and the body dries out. It has a cheesy smell, caused by butyric acid, and this smell attracts a new suite of corpse organisms. The surface of the body that is in contact with the ground becomes covered with mould as the body ferments.*" Ibid, http://www.deathonline.net/decomposition/decomposition/butyric_fermentation.htm. Personally, I have also had this stage of decomposition described to me as the fragrance of a "fresh baked pastry" by those who work with the deceased bodies alongside funeral homes. It could be assumed that as the body decomposes and ferments, the odor changes from a foul smell to a milder fragrance.

5   "Mummification is typically the end result of tissue, usually skin, with no nutritional value, which has survived the active decay process and is formed by the dehydration or desiccation of the tissue. Remaining skin is converted into a leathery or parchment-like sheet which clings to bone. Mummification most commonly develops in conditions of dry heat or in areas that have very low humidity, such as in arctic regions or deserts." Arpad A. Vass, "Beyond the Grave—Understanding Human Decomposition," *Microbiology Today*, http://www.sgm.ac.uk/pubs/micro_today/pdf/110108.pdf; http://www.deathonline.net/decomposition/resources/index.htm.

6   "29687 4750.07/The jackal...is smaller than a large dog, has a moderately bush tail, and is reddish brown with dark shadings above. It is cowardly and nocturnal. Like the fox, it is destructive to poultry, grapes, and vegetables, but is less fastidious, and readily devours the remains of others' feasts. Jackals generally go about in small companies. Their peculiar howl may frequently be heard in the evening and at any time in the night. It begins with a high-pitched, long-draw-out-cry. This is repeated two or three times, each time in a higher key than before. Finally there are several short, loud, yelping barks. Often when one raises the cry others join in. Jackals are not infrequently confounded with foxes. They breed freely with dogs." 29680 4750//4750 Jackal; International Standard Bible Encyclopedia; *Bible Works*.

7   "59730 9089.04/Heb: '*Iyim* occurs in Isa. 13:21 and 34:14 and in Jer. 50:39, three of the passages cited for Heb: *tsiyim*. The King James Version referring to Heb: 'i, "island," renders "wild beasts of the islands" (Isa. 13:22). The Revised Version (British and American) has "wolves," margin "howling creatures;" compare Arabic 'anwa,' "to howl," and ibn-'awa' pr wawi, "jackal."; 59726 9089//9089 Wild Beast; .International Standard Bible Encyclopedia; *Bible Works.*

8   Psalm 51:1, 2, 10–12.

9   "2 Sam. 21:10 – Dropped – Rather "poured," the proper word for heavy rain Exo. 9:33. The "early rain," or heavy rain of autumn, usually began in October, so that Rizpah's devoted watch continued about six months. How rare rain was in harvest we learn from 1 Sam. 12:17-18; Pro 26:1. The reason of the bodies being left unburied, contrary to Deut. 21:23, probably was that the death of these men being an expiation of the guilt of a violated oath, they were to remain until the fall of rain should give the assurance that God's anger was appeased, and the national sin forgiven." Barnes; *E-Sword.*

10 Lee Strobel, *The Case for Faith* (Grand Rapids, MI: Zondervan, 2000), 33.

11 Philip Yancey, *Disappointment with God: Three Questions No One Asks Aloud* (Grand Rapids, MI: Zondervan, 1988), 186.

12 Lee Strobel, *The Case for Faith,* 46–7.

13 John W. James and Frank Cherry, *The Grief Recovery Handbook: A Step-by-Step Program for Moving Beyond Loss* (New York: Harper & Row, 1988), 4.

14 Tim Hansel, *You Gotta Keep Dancin'* (Colorado Springs, CO: Victor Cook Communications, 1985), 35.

15 Ibid.

16 "Rock. 2. In Scripture, figurative, defense; means of safety; protection; strength; asylum. The Lord is my rock. 2 Sam. 22. 3. Firmness; a firm or immovable foundation." Definition for "Rock" Webster; *E-Sword.*

17 "Then Death and Hades were cast into the lake of fire. This is the second death. And anyone not found written in the Book of Life was cast into the lake of fire." (Revelation 20:14–15)

18 "And forgive us our sins, for we also forgive everyone who is indebted to us. And do not lead us into temptation, but deliver us from the evil one." (Luke 11:4)

19 W. V. Grant, *Growing Faith, Book Three of Divine Healing Answers,* vol. 1 (Dallas, TX: W. V. Grant),

Faith's Epilogue

THE HIDDEN POWER OF UNDEFEATABLE FAITH

Faith's Reward

When Destiny Hits the Mark

David was told what she had done, this Rizpah daughter of Aiah and con-
cubine of Saul. He then went and got the remains of Saul and Jonathan his
son from the leaders at Jabesh Gilead.... He gathered up their remains and
brought them together with the dead bodies of the seven who had just
been hanged. The bodies were taken back to the land of Benjamin and
given a decent burial in the tomb of Kish, Saul's father.

They did everything the king ordered to be done. That cleared things up:
from then on God responded to Israel's prayers for the land.
— 2 Samuel 21:11–14 (The Message)

Just as suddenly as the large raindrops had soaked her tunic and literally
splashed against the rock, they quickly transitioned from a few heavy
drops to a deluge. Rizpah wept openly with words of praise to Jehovah, as
within minutes veritable streams of water began to flow from the top of
the hillsides of Gibeah to the dry land and weary people of Israel. She
burst into a song of praise with tears of rejoicing, lifting her hands to
heaven, waving them before the Lord, and dancing to the melodious
strains of joy that filled her heart.

Singing, she proclaimed, "You have turned my mourning into dancing, O Lord. You have removed my sackcloth and clothed me with joy! You have been my hiding place and protected me from trouble. You have surrounded me with songs of deliverance. You are my Deliverer. Many are the woes of the wicked, but the Lord's unfailing love surrounds the woman who trusts in Him."

"Jehovah, You have opened the heavens and showered down blessings upon Your people, upon me, and upon the land. My heart sings to You and will not be silent. O Lord my God, I will give You thanks forever and ever! I will exalt You, O Lord, for You lifted me out of the depths of despair; You created in me a pure heart and renewed a steadfast spirit within me. I called to You for help and You heard me. Weeping may remain for a night, but rejoicing comes in the morning. For You take delight in Your people and crown the humble with salvation. Pour O heavens; pour out your blessings upon the land and the servants of the Lord!"[1]

Then much to Rizpah's surprise, what she thought to be thunder coming over the hill was a small regiment of King David's men on horseback. It wasn't the usual two replacements that came every few weeks to give reprieve to the guards on duty; it was a small regiment of soldiers. Since the rain started, she had been so consumed with rejoicing that she had lost track of space and time. She was so accustomed to the guards who always remained at a reasonable distance that she rarely paid attention to them or they to her.

But to see such a number of soldiers startled Rizpah; it instantly silenced her praises, piqued her curiosity, and nearly expunged her sense of security in one fell swoop. What were they here for, and what were they going to do? Her eyes darted to a cart being pulled behind two of the horses in the company. It had a dark tarp covering over it. She immediately flashed back to six months ago, when these same familiar faces carried her beloved sons and the grandsons of Saul to the crest of this hill with wood beams for crosses.... Now what were they up to?

The captain of the guard approached Rizpah with caution, with an unusual sense of reverence about his gait. He was tall and rugged looking, but had a commanding presence. If he had the mind to do so, he could have flung her frail body off the ridge like a boy tossing a river rock downstream. Her nervous intercessions became soundless as he approached; she could feel her body shiver under her wet garments and her knees began to buckle. She commanded herself to stand tall while doing her best to not look threatened by this captain of the king. Even though her hair was matted, her body frail, and the circles under eyes clearly indicated many sleepless days and nights these past six months, Rizpah still had a fire in her bones and a faith in her heart that Jehovah God was her rear guard. He would let nothing come her way that He would not give her the grace to handle.

Everything and everyone seemed to be moving in slow motion around her. Though her mind was racing to take it all in, her body felt faint. Near yet still at a comfortable distance, the captain dropped to one knee and removed his helmet while positioning it respectfully over his heart. He bowed his head and then looked up to face her with caring brown eyes. With his helmet in his hand and rain now dripping from his curly black hair, Rizpah's mind instantly flashed to her once beautiful Armoni, as he slowly unrolled a scroll.

With a deep resonating voice he said, "I bring this message to you from David, King of Israel." He then stood and began to read:

To Rizpah, daughter of Aiah and concubine of Saul. News of your faithful watch on behalf of Israel has come before me. I honor you and the house of Saul, as Jehovah's rains of refreshing now fall upon our land. I have ordered that the remains of Saul and Jonathan his son be brought, along with the remains of your beloved sons and the grandsons of Saul, to the burial cave of Kish, Saul's father, in the country of Benjamin in Zelah. There they will be buried as sons of King Saul and sons of Israel. They will be honored in death more than in life. For greater love has no man than this, than to lay down his life for the people of his nation.[2] And to you, dear mother, no mother has ever given more for her nation. For Armoni and Mephibosheth were their father's sons, but they were tender and only beloved in your sight their dear mother.[3] May your days of mourning be over and may your days of rejoicing begin. Your sons' lives will be honored alongside of kings and princes; they have made their mark on history by their great sacrifice. You, daughter, have served destiny and now destiny serves you. Your story will be told in generations to come. Loyalty that goes beyond death, trust that exalts the Lord God, and faith that remains undefeatable will not go without reward or without notice in the annals of history. Arise in your heart, dear mother in Israel, walk tall, for today you have become a firebrand in the hand of the Lord and made a mark in history that shall not be forgotten.

With that, the captain turned and gave orders to his men to remove the bodies of Rizpah's sons and the grandsons of Saul from the crosses. As he did, Rizpah, awestruck by what had just been said and the gracious manner in which it had been said, collapsed like a fragile flower in a rainstorm onto her faithful rock of intercession. With the words of the aged Phoebe ringing in her ears, *"Rizpah, you will hit the mark designed for you...you will hit the mark designed for you..."* she wept uncontrollably with tears of relief and gratefulness. Her life had made a difference; she had hit the mark. Her sons' lives had made a difference; they were destiny's claim. All was well with the world once again.

She then lifted her head to see the soldiers removing the bodies from the crosses, doing so with such careful reverence that waves of awe and gratefulness swept over her soul once again, evoking yet more tears. Once they had removed the bodies, with painstaking care they wrapped them in a cloth bearing the insignia of Saul's house and placed them in individual wicker caskets. They then carried them to the covered cart and laid them alongside two brass boxes with the insignia of the house of Saul on them, the ashes of Saul and Jonathan his son.⁴ At long last her boys would be granted the honor and dignity of men born of a royal line. They were now recognized as princes among men.

The captain of the guard returned to Rizpah and invited her to ride on the bench of the cart to the gravesite of Kish in nearby Zelah. Bowing her head in honor of his station and his kindness, she accepted the offer, desiring to see her sons' bodies reach their final resting place.

Rizpah pondered quietly as she rode—she was going to Zelah in the country of Benjamin, and *Benjamin* meant "blessing." The name Benjamin in the ancient scrolls represented "son of the right hand,"⁵ and the right hand of God always symbolized blessing. Blessing was upon her! The rock of her intercession had propelled her into the land of blessing. She could feel her heart beginning to race with joy. What a journey she was on! The soldiers she was in company with had no idea. This was no journey of burial, mourning, and gloom; it was an excursion into destiny, a triumphal procession of faith.

As the cart continued to roll down the muddy road and the rain continued to fall with joyful exuberance, it washed the black dirt of months on a desolate summit from her tired face and hands. Putting the wonderment of the effects of rain aside, her thoughts once again went to old Phoebe's prophetic declaration: *"Rizpah, you will hit the mark designed for you."* This time the Presence of Jehovah seemed to underscore her name. She suddenly became clearly aware that she was no longer pavement to be walked on; she was indeed a hot fiery coal, now strategically placed on the tip of an arrow just about to hit the mark designed for her.

As Rizpah's thoughts continued to meander along with the delightfully muddy pathway before her, she began to recall some of the name lessons that Phoebe had taught her so long ago. Much to her own amazement, she recalled that *Kish* meant "bow." Instantly, tears of rejoicing filled her eyes once again with the realization that she, God's hot fiery coal on the tip of God's arrow, was about to be placed in the "bow" of Kish, and she would indeed hit the mark designed for her! Before she could stop her mouth, she shouted out, *"Glory to God!"*

The guard next to her guiding the horses startled a bit, as did the horses. Then all three pretended to ignore her as she continued. She had ceased to care what guards or anyone else thought of her long ago, so his brief look of surprise could not stop the praises in her mouth.

"Jehovah, I cried out to You, and You heard my prayers. I waited patiently for You, and You heard my cry. You brought me up out of a horrible pit, out of the miry clay, and set my feet upon a rock, and established my steps. You have put a new song in my mouth—praise to You, Jehovah. Many will see Your faithfulness and rejoice and renew their trust in You, O Most High! Glory and honor be to Your Name!" [6]

In the midst of her praises, the horses drew to a stop. The cave of Kish was before them. Much to Rizpah's surprise, King David and another small regiment of soldiers were standing near the cave. The soldier sitting next to her settled the horses and then stepped down from the cart. The captain of the guard, who so reminded her of her firstborn son, was immediately by her side, offering his hand to help her down.

As he escorted her near the cave, her eyes met with King David's, and they both bowed simultaneously in honor of one another and the deceased. They stood facing the cave, her with her filthy and rain-soaked tunic and David in his kingly attire. They both patiently and quietly waited as the soldiers rolled away the stone that covered the entrance. Then two by two the soldiers carried the brass boxes with the ashes of Saul and his son into the cave, and then the wicker caskets of Rizpah's sons and the grandsons of Saul followed.

David stepped into the cave and bowed in honor of King Saul and Jonathan, his beloved friend. He had honored Saul in life, and now he honored him in death. He had also sworn an oath to Jonathan of undying friendship to him and to his house. How could he have not been here at this pivotal point in history? As he pondered the depths of his love for his friend Jonathan, sorrow overcame him and he wept uncontrollably as a beloved brother would.

Rizpah stood nearby but just outside the mouth of the cave, not wanting to overstep her boundaries and in honor of David's station and his great loss. Her focus shifted from David's sorrow to the wicker caskets, and she watched as her sons were laid carefully next to the ashes of the king. She then stepped back from the entrance of the cave, bowing to the ground in humility and gratefulness in honor of her dear Armoni and Mephibosheth. Her sacrifice was now embraced in honor as the "arrow" and the "bow" met.

Tears flooded Rizpah's eyes, and praises sprang forth from her mouth in quiet tones. "I give thanks to You, O Most High. I bow my head in honor, while my heart rejoices in Your lovingkindness and Your faithfulness. You, O Lord, have made me glad; I will forever triumph in the works of Your hands. O Lord, how great and thoughtful are Your works! Your thoughts are very deep. A senseless man does not know, nor does a fool understand this. But You, Lord, are on high forevermore. You have exalted me and mine, and I have been anointed with fresh oil. You are my Rock, and there is no unrighteousness in You! All glory and honor be unto Your Name!" [7]

As she took a breath and her praises ceased momentarily, she could feel the hem of King David's royal tunic brush against her hair. She lifted her head, and then he stopped and offered his hand to help her up. Humbled by his presence, she bowed her head again. He lifted her chin with his hand and looked into her eyes. With pools of tears filling his eyes and falling from his countenance, he said, "Thank you, dear Rizpah, loyal mother of Israel. Your faithfulness to the honor of Saul's house has opened the heavens, and showers of blessing are upon us once again. Go in peace and live out your days with the respect of your king and the gratefulness of your nation." With that, he turned and mounted his horse and rode toward Jerusalem with his company of men.

With peace of heart, Rizpah returned to the house of Saul to remain there for the rest of her days in comfort, under the protection of David's men. Upon hearing of her vigil and David's response to it, her servants returned and served her in quietness and contentment all the days of her life. She had been hidden away in poverty as a child by an abusive father, and in the house of Saul in a concubine's quarters. Then she had been hidden away on a lonely rock by an uncaring nation.

Now she was back on the quiet hillside of Gibeah. Only later, in her quiet moments, did she come to realize that she had been under the watchful eye of her heavenly Father all along. She had not really been hidden on a desolate summit at all, or on the street corner, or Saul's house, but rather she had been tucked away protectively under the shadow of Jehovah's wing because she was the apple of His eye.[8] Hidden away on a hillside to most perhaps, but never far from the watchful eye of her Maker.

At least one day a week, usually three, Rizpah would trek down the hillside unobtrusively and go into the city, back to the streets of her childhood. She would park herself on the corner of one of the market streets and share fruit and bread with the children of the streets while telling them stories of faith. As their eyes grew wide with wonder and their hearts filled with faith, her maids slipped soap and new tunics into their satchels. When she looked into their penetrating green or dancing brown eyes, she could not help but remember Armoni and Mephibosheth. Their legacy lived on through the stories she told and the children she ministered to. No longer would there be only one who would be "grand" or one who would "dispel the shame of Baal"—there would be *many* who would walk the streets with undefeatable faith in their hearts and a testimony in their mouths.

Rizpah never wore black again. She often donned regal purple or royal blue trimmed in silver, but her favorite and most often seen tunic was a deep crimson red trimmed in gold. It reminded her of the shed blood of her dear sons, who died for the sake of the kingdom and were buried in honor for their sacrifice. It also reminded her of who Jehovah made her to be, a "hot fiery coal on the tip of an arrow." She no longer shuffled along with her head held low as if she were worth nothing more than the earth upon which she walked. She walked in humility and gratefulness to a mighty God and in dignity, with purpose and anointing. When she wore her crimson dress, she could almost always have been seen dancing somewhere, in a field full of flowers or on her portico, sometimes even down the streets of her childhood. She was like the piper who piped and the children followed. Why? Because God had turned her mourning into dancing. He had removed her sackcloth and clothed her with a gladness that could not be restrained.

When Rizpah was too old to dance or make her trek down the hillside and up again, she took an apartment in the city with her two old maids by her side. It was there that destiny hit the mark over and over again and faith had its reward. Time and time again the now-grown children of the street would come to the door of the aged Rizpah and kneel by her bed-side, while their own dear children stood shyly at the door. They came for one purpose and one purpose only—to have her frail hand laid upon their heads and to hear words such as these: "The light of Jehovah goes before you. That which you have been crying out for will be yours, but in ways different than you planned or imagined."

Then stroking their faces and lifting their chins so that their eyes could meet, with tenderness she would continue, "Jehovah's ways are higher than your ways. You must not question, but rather stand strong, for Jehovah is with you and will be by your side. Your hope will be found on a Rock. Though your sacrifice will be great, know that no sacrifice goes unnoticed by Jehovah, the Rock of your salvation."

With tears filling her eyes and theirs as well, she would go on. "The Most High God goes before you and prepares the way. He will be with you and will watch over you. He will comfort you and hear your cry. He will answer your prayers and the prayers of generations to come. You will hit the mark designed for you. Go on your way, call upon the all-wise One— Jehovah will be with you."

Though her body became too frail to dance, dancing never left Rizpah's eyes. They told of a joy that superseded any despair mankind could face and sparkled with a dance of joy that could not be compared to any that the world had to offer. Her eyes were radiant with the light of Jehovah, so much so that people drew close just to see the sparkle, the delight, the joy, and the wonder they beheld. Though her voice became weak, it always spoke with the tenderness and wisdom of God. Though her natural strength diminished, her faith grew stronger, while her joy grew deeper and her laughter lighter. There was a joy and a fiery anointing in this grand old woman; it was an undeniable faith that was absolutely undefeatable. She had been to the depths of despair and back again, and nothing could penetrate the faith that she held dear to her heart. That faith released in her a joy that was infectious and a testimony that was unsurpassed.

Tears of sorrow never filled Rizpah's eyes again, only tears that came from moments of laughter and joy. It was laughter that filled her house, her heart, and all those who came for a visit; but it was not a laughter that was fleeting, here one moment and gone the next. It was a laughter that penetrated the heart and engraved joy onto the soul. With a faith that was invincible, she had a joy that was not only infectious, but was also impenetrable to the demons of hell. Though the natural surroundings of her last days were humble, she was rich in spirit, and it was this spirit she gave as a gift to all who crossed her threshold.

This aged, fiery, anointed woman of God died in faith surrounded by friends, with a smile on her face that told those who stood nearby that her Maker and Lover of her soul had come and escorted her in to Abraham's bosom. Her story had been untraditional and her burial gown was as well. It was her favorite crimson red trimmed in gold, representative of the firebrand calling of God on her life and the blood that was shed for her and her nation. Her veil, chosen by those who dearly loved her, was white, symbolizing the life she lived as a pure white arrow of sacrifice and love, in contrast to the blackness of the days in which she made her greatest sacrifice. Rizpah had hit the target destined for her with precision, joy, and faith that was undefeatable. She died with a knowing smile on her face and was buried near a rock on a crest on the hillsides of Gibeah, the place of her greatest challenge and consummate victory.

Can you see Rizpah dancing? Can you feel her joy? Can you see the target of her destiny blazing with the fiery-tipped arrow that made its dead-center mark? Can you sense the excitement of destiny being renewed within yourself? As we live humble, obedient lives, no matter what sacrifice we are asked to make, the Lord will ultimately honor our sacrifice and bless us—even if it's at the graveside or in the life hereafter.

After Rizpah's personal sacrifice of pain and suffering was honored by David, the rains of blessing came upon that sacrifice—because though she stood alone on a Rock, she stood in one accord with her nation. When the wages of sin were paid through the sacrifice of substitutionary death, the blessing of God came down. Rains of refreshing and healing began to fall; the land was blessed and the famine was over. The rain fell on Rizpah, on her sacrifice, and on the people. They stood in solidarity before a just and holy God.

Rizpah, like Mary, let her seed fall to the ground and die that it might rise again and bring forth more fruit. Rizpah's sons and the grandsons of Saul died so that one generation might be restored to blessing. Jesus died so that all generations might have the opportunity to be redeemed.

Even though our life goals may not be attained in the way we might prefer or in the timing we desire, God will always bless obedience. He loves to mold and shape obedience into undefeatable faith and then use it to affect the lives of others. If Rizpah's story tells us anything, it's that God honors obedience and sacrifice with abundant blessing. It tells us that He will work out His marvelous plan in our lives even if life events twist and turn it around. It tells us that He not only cares for us personally, but He cares for communities and nations as well. It tells us that His vision is bigger than ours is. It tells us that our individual lives count and that our responses to the details of our daily lives count. Our sacrifices matter to Him and to others. The bottom line is that your responses count, and your life counts. I would rather make my life count than merely count my days. Wouldn't you? As difficult or as small and insignificant as you or your life situation may seem, it matters to God.

There is something in fact, very special about life itself, but many people miss it by virtue of trying to wrap their finite brains around the mind of the Creator of the universe. "In the natural world, human beings only receive about 30 percent of the light spectrum.... In the supernatural realm, our vision is even more limited, and we get only occasional glimpses of that unseen world." [9] If our vision and hearing is that limited in the natural, what makes us think that we can understand the will and ways of God enough to direct Him in how to handle the affairs of our life or the lives of others?

You may know yourself, but your knowledge is limited to what you know about yourself since your arrival on this earth and not beyond your departure from it. Jeremiah 1:5 says, "Before I shaped you in the womb, I knew all about you. Before you saw the light of day, I had holy plans for you..." *(The Message)*. God knew you before you were even conceived, and He knows what you will be doing following your earthly departure. When Job cried out in the anguish of his soul, he cursed the day he was born:

"Obliterate the day I was born. Blank out the night I was conceived! Let it be a black hole in space. May God above forget it ever happened. Erase it from the books! May the day of my birth be buried in deep darkness, shrouded by the fog, swallowed by the night.... What's the point of life when it doesn't make sense, when God blocks all the roads to meaning?... The worse of my fears has come true, what I've dreaded most has happened. My repose is shattered, my peace destroyed. No rest for me, ever— death has invaded life.... Oh, if only someone would give me a hearing! I've signed my name to my defense—let the Almighty One answer!" [10]

One of Job's insensitive, but momentarily insightful, friends responded, "If God is silent, what's that to you? If he turns his face away, what can you do about it? But whether silent or hidden, he's there, ruling, so that those who hate God won't take over and ruin people's lives." [11]
Then God spoke to Job:

"Why do you confuse the issue? Why do you talk without knowing what you're talking about? Pull yourself together, Job! Up on your feet! Stand tall! I have some questions for you, and I want some straight answers. Where were you when I created the earth? Tell me since you know so much! Who decided on its size? Certainly you'll know that! Who came up with the blueprints and measurements? How was its foundation poured, and who set the cornerstone, while the morning stars sang in chorus and all the angels shouted praise? And who took charge of the ocean when it gushed forth like a baby from the womb? That was me! I wrapped it in soft clouds, and tucked it in safely at night. Then I made a playpen for it, a strong playpen so it couldn't run loose, and said, 'Stay here, this is your place. Your wild tantrums are confined to this place.' And have you ever ordered Morning, 'Get up!' Told Dawn, 'Get to work!'" [12]

God continued with detailed description of the wonders of the earth, as well as offering Job an amazing zoology lesson. He then concluded His allocution with no further explanation other than the vastness of His greatness, as if to say, "If you were around here when I created all of this, then perhaps I might feel obligated to explain to you the whys of everything I do and allow. But you weren't, so I don't. Just trust that I am all-knowing, all-powerful, and ever-watchful." Job wisely and humbly responded with a prayer of repentance for his presumption and a confession of his complete and utter trust in the Creator of the Universe.

In our overconcern for the whys of the details of our lives, as well as our overemphasis on what we deem to be important, we often overlook and minimize the elemental value of life itself. Though God cares deeply about the details of our lives and the depths of our pain and suffering, He cares most about our hearts and how we will use the pain for His glory. C. S. Lewis once said, "God whispers to us in our pleasures, speaks in our conscience, but shouts in our pains. It is his megaphone to rouse a deaf world." [13]

God wants us to use everything that life has given us for His glory. Not everything that comes our way is glorious, but everything can be used for His glory. Our perspectives are so finite, so limited to the confines of this earth; we need desperately to seek His perspective and trust His leading. Give up insisting on explanations and visible proofs of His watchful eye. When God seems absent, He may be closer than He's ever been.

The truth is that life is invigorating as well as deplorable, fulfilling as well as frustrating, sweet as well as bitter, and everything in between. Every valley does have a mountain, every low has a high, every back has a front, and every bottom has a top. God wants us to embrace it all and require it to mold us and shape us into the person that He wants us to be. To allow life to make us into a vessel worthy of carrying the very Presence of God to others who are wounded and hurting is a great honor regardless of the cost. True faith does not attempt to persuade God to do our will our way as much as it positions us to do His will.

"This time called life is far more sacred and special than any of us can ever imagine. Out task, or should I say our privilege, is to become aware of it and to participate as deeply and as fully as we are capable." [14] Now is as good a time as any to jump into life, to be that fiery coal on the tip of God's arrow, placed in His bow, hitting with precision the target designed for you. Participate as you never have before in life, with joy and anticipation. God wants you to enjoy the journey and to trust in His sincere care, as well as His knowledge of the bigger picture. Embrace life and fear not, for you serve a God who is invincible, undefeatable, and completely on your side. "His plans are to prosper you, not to harm you, they are plans with a bright hope for a fulfilling future." [15] Go for it; make your mark on history. Great will be your reward when destiny hits the mark through you.

The Who and the Why of Trust

2 SAMUEL 22:3: *"The God of my strength, in whom I will trust; my shield and the horn of my salvation, my stronghold and my refuge; my Savior, You save me from violence."*

2 SAMUEL 22:31: *"As for God, His way is perfect; the word of the LORD is proven; he is a shield to all who trust in Him."*

PSALM 2:12: *"Blessed are all those who put their trust in Him."*

PSALM 5:11: *"But let all those rejoice who put their trust in You; let them ever shout for joy, because You defend them; let those also who love Your name be joyful in You."*

PSALM 9:10: *"And those who know Your name will put their trust in You; for You, LORD, have not forsaken those who seek You."*

PSALM 18:2: *"The LORD is my rock and my fortress and my deliverer; my God, my strength, in whom I will trust; my shield and the horn of my salvation, my stronghold."*

PSALM 18:30: *"As for God, His way is perfect; the word of the LORD is proven; he is a shield to all who trust in Him."*

PSALM 31:19: *"Oh, how great is Your goodness, which You have laid up for those who fear You, which You have prepared for those who trust in You in the presence of the sons of men!"*

PSALM 36:7: *"How precious is Your lovingkindness, O God! Therefore the children of men put their trust under the shadow of Your wings."*

PSALM 37:3: *"Trust in the LORD, and do good; dwell in the land, and feed on His faithfulness."*

PSALM 52:8: *"But I am like a green olive tree in the house of God; I trust in the mercy of God forever and ever."*

PSALM 56:3: *"Whenever I am afraid, I will trust in You."*

PSALM 56:11: *"In God I have put my trust; I will not be afraid. What can man do to me?"*

PSALM 62:8: *"Trust in Him at all times, you people; pour out your heart before Him; God is a refuge for us. Selah."*

PSALM 118:8: *"It is better to trust in the LORD than to put confidence in man."*

PSALM 119:42: *"So shall I have an answer for him who reproaches me, for I trust in Your word."*

PSALM 125:1: *"Those who trust in the LORD are like Mount Zion, which cannot be moved, but abides forever."*

PSALM 143:8: *"Cause me to hear Your lovingkindness in the morning, for in You do I trust; cause me to know the way in which I should walk, for I lift up my soul to You."*

PROVERBS 3:5–6: *"Trust in the LORD with all your heart, and lean not on your own understanding; in all your ways acknowledge Him, and He shall direct your paths."*

PROVERBS 28:25: *"He who is of a proud heart stirs up strife, but he who trusts in the LORD will be prospered."*

PROVERBS 29:25: *"The fear of man brings a snare, but whoever trusts in the LORD shall be safe."*

PROVERBS 30:5: *"Every word of God is pure; he is a shield to those who put their trust in Him."*

ISAIAH 12:2: *"Behold, God is my salvation, I will trust and not be afraid; 'For YAH, the LORD, is my strength and song; he also has become my salvation.'"*

2 CORINTHIANS 1:9: *"Yes, we had the sentence of death in ourselves, that we should not trust in ourselves but in God who raises the dead."*

NOTES

1   Paraphrased excerpts adapted from Psalm 30, 32, 51.

2   Paraphrase adapted from John 15:13.

3   Paraphrase adapted from Proverbs 4:3.

4   "The day after the battle of Gilboa the Philistines plundered the battlefield, making off with jewelry, weapons, and anything else of value. As they did so they came on the bodies of Saul and his sons, evidently identified by clothing, insignia, and seals hung about their necks or in waist pouches. They cut off Saul's head and probably those of his sons and took off their body armor and deposited all of this as trophies in the temple of Ashtoreth, the female deity worshiped beside Dagon.... The Philistines fastened the bodies of the four to the wall of Beth Shan, standing just east of the battlefield a.... When the men in Jabesh Gilead on the east bank heard it, they felt duty-bound to do something for the benefactor who had rescued them from their plight (1 Samuel 11:1–11). They journeyed through the night and stole the bodies of Saul and his sons and brought them back to Jabesh Gilead. Verse 12 states that they 'burned' the bodies, according to most translations..." Howard Vos, *New Illustrated Bible Manners and Customs* (Nashville, TN: Thomas Nelson, 1999), 193.

5   "01277 550 Benjamin; 10278 550.01 ("son of my right hand"), as Jacob named him; first called by his dying mother Rachel Benoni, son of my sorrow." Fausset; *Bible Works.*

6   Paraphrase adapted from Psalm 40:1–3.

7   Paraphrase adapted from Psalm 92.

8   Paraphrase of Psalm 17:8.

9   Philip Yancey, *Disappointment with God: Three Questions No One Asks Aloud* (Grand Rapids: MI: Zondervan, 1988), 236.

10   Job 3:1–3, 23, 25, 26; 31:35, 36, *The Message.*

11   Job 34:29–30, *The Message.*

12   Job 38:1–13, *The Message.*

13   C. S. Lewis, *The Problem of Pain* (New York: Macmillan, 1962), 93.

14   Tim Hansel, *You Gotta Keep Dancin'* (Colorado Springs, CO: Victor Cook Communications, 1985), 73.

15   Paraphrase of Jeremiah 29:11.

Faith's Challenge

What About You?

Now faith is the substance of things hoped for, the evidence of things not seen. — Hebrews 11:1

I do not presume to have the call or the anointing of the late Kathryn Kuhlman. However, I must agree with her statement, as a testimony to my own walk of faith: "I am not a woman with great faith—I am a woman with a little faith in the Great God!"[1] Having even "a little faith" in a "Great God" can mold and shape you and me into people of undefeatable faith.

WHAT IS FAITH?

What does it mean to be a person of undefeatable faith? What is faith's challenge to you and me? The Bible has a lot to say about faith:

There are 667 direct references to faith in the Bible, 193 in the Old Testament and 474 in the New. Jesus referred to faith and belief 156 times in all 4 Gospels (24 times in Matthew, 21 times in Mark, 25 times in Luke, and 87 times in John's gospel.) The apostle Paul refers to faith and belief 192 times in his letters. The other writers refer to faith 69 times. Faith verses are found 53 times in Luke's account of the Acts of the Apostles. The epistle with the most references to faith is Paul's letter to the Romans with 50 references to faith in only 16 chapters. That averages just over 3 references per chapter. His 2 letters to his spiritual son, Timothy, are a close second with 32 comments about faith or belief in only 10 chapters. The Bible is full of faith.[2]

"Faith is the substance of things hoped for, the evidence of things not seen."

The only New Testament scripture that actually defines faith is Hebrews 11:1. It says that "Faith is the substance of things hoped for," the very essence of things that are saturated with hope. Faith is "the evidence of things not seen." Hence, when an obvious answer to prayer is not seen, faith is the evidence that the answer is still on the way. Once the answer arrives, faith is no longer required; gratefulness is activated and faith awaits its next challenge.

Hebrews 11:2 says, "This [faith] is what the ancients were commended for" (NIV). This is a reference to the heroes of faith in the Old Testament being commended by the Lord for their faith, which was those things they could not see and yet still believed would come to pass. That was their level of faith, and it pleased the Lord. There is a distinct difference between our belief in God and our faith in Him. Many people believe that there is a God who rules and reigns, but they lack a personal faith in Him. There are also many who believe in God and have a personal faith in Him, but have not received faith from Him to believe that they can hear His voice or that He can do miracles today. This is usually because it is not something they have been taught from the Word of God or they believe is possible today. What about you? Where are you on this spectrum?

In his book *The Real Faith*, Dr. Charles Price says:

What a mistake it is to take our *belief* in God and call it *faith*.... There is a great deal of difference between what we call the *faith of man in God,* and the *faith of God* that is imparted to man. Such faith is not the child of effort neither is it born of struggle. If it is the faith *of* God, then we get if *from* Him, and not from our mental attitudes or affirmations. Jesus did not say, "If you have the power to believe that God will remove that mountain, then He will do it." Neither did He say, "If you can believe hard enough that it is done, then it will be done." But He did say, *"Have the faith of God."* In other words, get some of God's faith; and then when you have that, you will have the only power with which mountains can be moved and cast into the sea." [3]

The challenge Dr. Price makes begs a response. Believers must not only cleave to their personal faith in Jesus Christ as Lord and Savior, but also beseech God to impart His faith to them. God can and certainly does do miracles apart from the involvement of any persons. However, it is clear in the New Testament that He desires and delights in using those who believe in Him as channels of His love and power, but to be used by Him effectively, one must "have the faith of God," [4] not just faith in Him. Hence, it is only by a divine deposit from God that miracles can flow through the believer to others.

✦ Evangelist Kathryn Kuhlman said, "Faith is that quality or power by which the things desired become the things possessed.... You cannot weigh it or confine it to a container; it is not something that you can take out and look at and analyze; you cannot definitely put your finger on it and positively say, 'This is it.' To explain it precisely and succinctly is almost like trying to define energy in one comprehensive statement.... If your faith is powerless, it is not faith. You cannot have faith without results any more than you can have motion without movement. The thing we sometimes call faith, is only trust, but although we trust in the Lord, it is faith which has action and power." [5]

+ Pastor Wendell Smith says, "Faith is the most powerful force in the universe because it bridges the unknown and the known, heaven and earth, eternity and time."[6]

+ Author Tim Hansel says, "Faith isn't really faith until it's all that you're holding on to.... Faith plus nothing equals that which pleases God."[7]

+ Author Bob George says, "The value of faith is found in the object of that faith [Jesus], not in faith itself."[8]

+ Preacher, writer, and intercessor E. M. Bounds made these statements about faith: "When faith ceases to pray, it ceases to live.... Prayer projects faith on God and God on the world. Only God can move mountains, but faith and prayer move God.... Faith is a consciousness of the divine, an experienced communion, a realized certainty.... Faith is the foundation of Christian character and the security of the soul.... The faith which creates powerful praying is the faith which centers itself on a powerful person.... Yet faith is called upon, and that right often to wait in patience before God, and is prepared for God's seeming delays in answering prayer. Faith does not grow disheartened because prayer is not immediately honored; it takes God at his Word, and lets him take what time he chooses in fulfilling his purposes, and in carrying on his work. There is bound to be much delay and long days of waiting for true faith, but faith accepts the conditions—knows there will be delays in answering prayer, and regards such delays as times of testing, in the which, it is privileged to show its mettle, and the stern stuff of which it is made.... Faith is an operation of God, a divine illumination, a holy energy implanted by the Word of God and the Spirit in the human soul—a spiritual, divine principle which takes of the supernatural and makes it a thing apprehendable by the faculties of time and sense.… Faith is not an aimless act of the soul, but a looking to God and a resting upon his promises. … Faith gives birth to prayer, grows stronger, strikes deeper, and rises higher in the struggles and wrestlings of mighty petitioning." [9]

✦ Author Gary Kinnaman says, "Faith is trust and confidence in another to do what you cannot do yourself." [10]

✦ Martin Luther said, "Reason is the greatest enemy that faith has." [11]

WHERE DOES FAITH COME FROM?

Romans 10:17 says, "So then faith comes by hearing, and hearing by the Word of God." Faith comes by hearing what? The Word of God.

1. Faith comes by Jesus, the Presence of the Word of God.
Who is the Word of God? According to John 1:1, 14 [12] and 1 John 1:1; [13] 5:7, [14] Jesus is the Word. Revelation 19:13 says, "He was clothed with a robe dipped in blood, and His name is called The Word of God." So faith comes by the very Presence of Jesus, who is the Word of God. Hence, faith is not so much about us having faith as it is about us knowing God. It is through knowing Him personally that the faith of God will be imparted. It is not faith we must seek; it is God. Far too many people confuse this issue and run hard after what they deem to be faith or people of faith, all the while missing the point that *what* they need to run to and *who* they need to run to is Jesus, the Christ.

As Pastor Wendell Smith says,

There is no problem He cannot solve.
There is no question He cannot answer.
There is no disease He cannot heal.
There is no demon He cannot cast out.

There is no enemy He cannot defeat.

There is no difficulty He cannot overcome.

There is no stronghold He cannot bring down.

There is no bondage He cannot break.

There is no prison He cannot open.

There is no need He cannot meet.

There is no mountain He cannot move.[15]

In other words, Jesus is the source of faith! So to try to drum up faith without His Presence is an act of futility. As right and compassionate as activating faith may seem, without acknowledging Who the miracle worker is and who the miracle worker isn't is pseudo-faith and is hollow and ineffective and usually ends up disappointing and hurting people in need of a genuine miracle. Only Jesus Christ performs miracles; people do not.

✦ **Jesus said,** *"I am the bread of life.* He who comes to Me shall never hunger, and he who believes in Me shall never thirst." (John 6:35)

✦ **Jesus said,** *"I am the light of the world.* He who follows Me shall not walk in darkness, but have the light of life." (John 8:12)

✦ **Jesus said,** *"I am the door.* If anyone enters by Me, he will be saved, and will go in and out and find pasture." (John 10:9)

✦ **Jesus said,** *"I am the good shepherd.* The good shepherd gives His life for the sheep." (John 10:11)

✦ **Jesus said,** *"I am the resurrection and the life.* He who believes in Me, though he may die, he shall live." (John 11:25)

✦ **Jesus said,** *"I am the way, the truth, and the life.* No one comes
to the Father except through Me." (John 14:6)

✦ **Jesus said,** *"I am the vine,* you are the branches. He who abides
in Me, and I in him, bears much fruit; for without Me you can
do nothing." (John 15:5)

As we continue to grow in faith, we must always remember who is the
Creator and who is the *created.* When that fact remains clear in our thinking, it is easy to give Him not only the glory, but the needs as well.

2.   Faith also comes from the Bible, the written Word of God.
Jesus is the Word of God, but He has also left His recorded Word for us to
receive from. Faith comes not only from His Presence, but also by the
hearing of His Word preached, as well as "hearing" it by reading and
meditating on it. E. M. Bounds confirms, "Faith grows by reading and
meditating upon the Word of God." [16]

Faith evangelist Kathryn Kuhlman says, "Faith is more than belief; it is
more than confidence; it is more than trust, and above all, it is never
boastful. If it is pure faith, Holy Ghost faith, it will never work contrary to
the Word of God, and neither will it work contrary to His wisdom and
will." [17] The only way to know for sure that you are not praying or
proclaiming something that is not contrary to the will of God is to know
what the Word of God says about that which concerns you. True people of
faith are students of the Word of God. If you want your faith to increase
with maturity, you must study the Word.

THE BIBLE CLEARLY SAYS:

PSALM 119:11: *"Your word have I hidden in my heart, that I might not
sin against You."*

PSALM 119:16: *"I will delight myself in Your statutes; I will not forget
Your word."*

PSALM 119:50: *"This is my comfort in my affliction, for Your word has given me life."*

PSALM 119:105: *"Your word is a lamp to my feet and a light to my path."*

PSALM 119:114: *"You are my hiding place and my shield; I hope in Your word."*

PSALM 119:140: *"Your word is very pure; therefore Your servant loves it."*

PSALM 119:160: *"The entirety of Your word is truth, and every one of Your righteous judgments endures forever."*

PSALM 119:162: *"I rejoice at Your word as one who finds great treasure."*

PSALM 119:172: *"My tongue shall speak of Your word, for all Your commandments are righteousness."*

PSALM 130:5: *"I wait for the LORD, my soul waits, and in His word I do hope."*

PSALM 138:2: *"I will worship toward Your holy temple, and praise Your name for Your lovingkindness and Your truth; for You have magnified Your word above all Your name."*

The Word of God is a powerful tool to be used in faith-filled prayer. God listens and responds to His mentioned promises. He is a promise-keeping God, and you cannot proclaim the many promises of the Bible if you do not know them. In His Word are promises of salvation, healing, strength, comfort, mercy, grace—the list goes on and on. If you have lost motivation to study the Word of God and yet yearn to be a person of faith, let your faith be renewed by fresh meditation on His Word.

Are there different levels or types of faith?

Yes, it does appear throughout the Bible that there are different types or levels of faith. Just as there are varying ministries that minister in different capacities, there are different realms of functioning faith within the body of Christ. For example, some pastors shepherd God's people as ordained pastors, some as lay leaders, some as small group leaders, some in the church, and some in the marketplace. Some Bible teachers teach as pastors/teachers in the church, some as classroom teachers in the church, some as Bible college teachers, some as seminary teachers, and some as one-on-one counseling teachers. One is not better than the other; all are meant to benefit and flow together with the other for the sake of Christ and His church.

Some of the obvious capacities in which faith functions through believers as outlined in the Bible are these:

1. **All true Christians have *a believing faith* in Christ as Lord and Savior. Habakkuk says, "The just shall live by his faith."**

   Romans 3:21–26 says, "But now the righteousness of God apart from the law is revealed, being witnessed by the Law and the Prophets, even the righteousness of God, through faith in Jesus Christ, to all and on all who believe. For there is no difference; for all have sinned and fall short of the glory of God, being justified freely by His grace through the redemption that is in Christ Jesus, whom God set forth as a propitiation by His blood, through faith, to demonstrate His righteousness, because in His forbearance God had passed over the sins that were previously committed, to demonstrate at the present time His righteousness, that He might be just and the justifier of the one who has faith in Jesus."

2. All believers have *a measure of faith.* What each individual has faith for or directed to may vary, but each has a portion of faith.

Romans 12:3–5 says, "For I say, through the grace give to me, to everyone who is among you, not to think of himself more highly than he ought to think, but to think soberly, as God has dealt to each one a measure of faith. For as we have many members in one body, but all the members do not have the same function, so we, being many, are one body in Christ, and individually members of one another."

3. Some believers have *a gift of faith.*

First Corinthians 12:4–11 says, "There are diversities of gifts, but the same Spirit. There are differences of ministries, but the same Lord. And there are diversities of activities, but it is the same God who works all in all. But the manifestation of the Spirit is given to each one for the profit of all: for to one is given the word of wisdom through the Spirit, to another the word of knowledge through the same Spirit, to another faith by the same Spirit, to another gifts of healings by the same Spirit, to another the working of miracles, to another prophecy, to another discerning of spirits, to another different kinds of tongues, to another the interpretation of tongues. But one and the same Spirit works all these things, distributing to each one individually as He wills."

4. All believers are to have *a spirit of faith,* or attitude of faith.

Second Corinthians 4:11–14 says, "For we who live are always delivered to death for Jesus' sake, that the life of Jesus also may be manifested in our mortal flesh. So then death is working in us, but life in you. And since we have the same spirit of faith, according to what is written, 'I believed and therefore I spoke,' we also believe and therefore speak, knowing that He who raised up the Lord Jesus will also raise us up with Jesus, and will present us with you."

5. All believers are able to have a *word of faith.*

Romans 10:8 says, "But what does it say? 'The word is near you, in your mouth and in your heart' (that is, the word of faith which we preach)."

WHAT DOES THIS MEAN FOR YOU?

What is your destiny?

So, faith is that which is not seen and yet is hoped for, it comes from the living Presence of Jesus and His Word, and there are different capacities and functions of faith. Now what about you? How does all of this relate to you and the principles of faith found in the story of our heroine, Rizpah? Who are you and what is your destiny? Rizpah had a destiny and a pathway. What pathway of faith has God destined for you to walk? Where are you living today? Are you in the valley, on the mountaintop, or somewhere in between? Are you at the beginning of your personal journey, in the middle, or near the supposed end?

Every season of life, every detailed occurrence of every day, serves to underscore the uniqueness of each life. Rizpah was unique; her journey was unique. So are you and yours. When it comes to human life, there is no such thing as ordinary. There is not one life or life story that is more significant than another, other than the life and story of Jesus Christ. He is set apart from us all as the One designated to die, once and for all, for all mankind, on a cruel cross. He is the God-man who came to redeem us from a life doomed to destruction and fruitlessness.

Rizpah was destined to be the mother of two sons sacrificed on behalf of her nation, as well as to be a fiery hot coal on the tip of God's arrow to hit a mark. Actually, we're all called to make a difference in this life, to hit the mark. Will you blaze through the air like a fiery hot coal and set a generation free from bondage? Will you embrace your bow of sacrifice and hit the mark of honor? Will the sacrifice you offer up to the Lord bring down rains of refreshing and healing for a person or a people? You're not called to do it the way Rizpah did, but you are called to obey God's voice and do whatever He tells you to do. You're called to do it the way God has destined for you to do it. What is your destiny? What is the dream that burns deep within you?

+ Is it to be the first person in your family to stay clean and sober?

+ Is it to be the first person in your family to actually walk out a forgiving lifestyle?

+ Is it to reach the hurting in your neighborhood that no one else will reach out to?

+ Is it to run for a political office?

+ Is it to parent godly children?

+ Is it to preach the gospel in many nations?

What do you see? What do you want to see in your future? Where is the courage to dream what you desperately want to dream? Where is the dream you once dreamed? What happened to it? Do not let circumstances of life convince you that you are nothing more than pavement to be walked on. Don't do it! Reach for faith; reach for the destiny that belongs to you. You have been called to be a fiery hot coal—a thunderbolt on the tip of an arrow. You have been destined to make a difference in this life, on this earth, in this generation. Whether you are to minister to one life or many, you have been destined to make a difference.

What's your name? *Pavement or thunderbolt?* Numerous people in the Bible had their names changed by God, and it changed their perspective on their destiny. It didn't change God's perspective—He knew their beginning from their ending before they were even conceived—but it changed theirs. Jacob changed from "the supplanter, a man who replaced another"[18] to Israel, "Prince." Sarai, "quarrelsome," changed to Sarah, "princess, mother of princes."[19] Saul, "asked for," was changed to Paul, "little."[20] (Paul was humble in his own eyes from the moment he encountered Jesus, but was great in God's eyes.)

What does your name mean? What does it mean to you? Can you see destiny in your name? Destiny is not wrapped up in a name per se, but it is amazing how often a name can indicate something worthy of consideration or prayer.

Regardless of your name and what it may mean, what is that you see in your future? What legacy would you like to leave for the next generation? How would you like to be remembered?

What is your heritage?

Rizpah's heritage, her family root system, was Aiah, "one who laments." She did not grow up in an atmosphere of faith, but she wasn't going to let that hold her back. She knew how to lament. She had grown up with woe, but she also knew how to remain on the Rock, being a good steward of what the Lord had given to her. She protected her sacrifice and the sacrifice of Israel until it was covered with dignity and honor. It was shameful for bodies to be left unburied in Rizpah's generation just as it is in ours. Rizpah would not leave her sacrifice in shame, to be devoured by the enemies of her faith. It was her constant vigil that actually shamed David into acknowledging her sacrifice publicly, and when he did, Israel's drought was turned into showers of blessing. Rizpah knew that only on the Rock would her mourning be turned into dancing, her sorrows into joy, and a divine exchange would be made on her behalf and on behalf of her nation.

What or who in your past has marked you or devalued you? What value have they attached to you? If it has been less than what the Word of God says about you, let it go. Discount it as ignorance, shortsightedness, or an inspiration from the pit of hell. Forgive and let the hurt go. It's holding you back from the journey God has ahead for you. If you have a past full of hurts and a present full of 'lamenting hawks,' forgive and release them. Hand over the keys of that emotional jail cell you have them in to Jesus. Remember that vengeance belongs to Him. Let Him take care of it. Nothing you can do or say will change the past or the negative present other than Jesus Christ, who comes to offer you a healed perspective and renewed joy. It is His peace, His joy, and His faith that cannot be touched or brought down by any insensitive unknowing person, a personal defeat, or any demon in hell.

Breakthrough is born in the womb of adversity. Undefeatable faith is born in the womb of adversity. Expect a miracle of healing for your wounded heart or your misguided perspective on your personal value...*today*. It's on the way; the miracle is in the womb of your heart. Stay close to the Word of God and to the Presence of God, for the miracle is very near. Remember that God's Word says you are His child, His creation, well planned and greatly loved. He thinks about you,[21] He loves you,[22] He enjoys you,[23] He designed you for a specific reason,[24] and you are a blessing to Him just as you are.[25]

The word *circumstance* comes from the root word *circum* which means "circle of your standing." Step out of the circle of your standing, and enlarge your borders in victory today. A hovering, "lamenting hawk" will not bind you anymore. As you reach out for God's Word and His Presence through the avenue of forgiveness and release, your heart is cleansed, the web that had you bound is cut, and you are free.

Where does your hope come from?

A key to continual freedom is to be found in answering this question: Is your hope in something temporal or in Someone eternal? Rizpah's hope rested initially on her sons. As precious as family relationships can be, each one is a temporal relationship apart from the eternal friendship we make with each other in the saving knowledge of our Lord Jesus Christ. In heaven there will be no husbands or wives, fathers or mothers, sons or daughters. We will all be brothers and sisters in Christ, children of our heavenly Father. You must not let your faith depend upon your relationships with friends or family. Faith is a personal, private decision between you and Christ. If your faith is based on a family member, it could be dashed upon a rock, just as Rizpah's was. If she hadn't had a personal faith in the living God, she would not have hit the target and brought honor to her sons or the nation of Israel.

In Luke 8:22–25, Jesus told His disciples, "Let's go over to the other side of the lake." The winds came up and the disciples awakened Jesus proclaiming, "Master, we are perishing!" Jesus, in turn, asked them the question, "Where is your faith?" He wanted them to acknowledge whether their faith was in Him or in the storm. Today He's still asking the same question: "Where is your faith?" He's asking it of you right now. Is your faith in a boat, in a storm, in a loss, or in the Master of your soul? Only Jesus is the Master of the storms of life; only He is the source of the undefeatable faith that you will need to continue your personal journey.

Trials provide the broken ground into which spiritual seeds can be planted. They are not to be resisted; they are to be embraced and given permission to do the work of God in you. It's human nature to resist a trial, but Christ wants to give you the grace to embrace the trial and grow and expand in ways that you never imagined you could. Life is what you have, not what you wish you could have. Live in peace and contentment where you are, all the while reaching for the future in faith. Don't spend your entire life preparing to live—live it today. Each day comes but once in human history. No matter how bad a day may be, there is always a treasure from the Lord, hidden in the darkness for your eyes only. Isaiah 45:2–3 says:

> "I will go before you and make the crooked places straight; I will break in pieces the gates of bronze and cut the bars of iron. I will give you the treasures of darkness and hidden riches of secret places, that you may know that I, the LORD, who call you by your name, am the God of Israel."

The "treasures of darkness and hidden riches of secret places" can only be found in those places where our natural instincts would never lead us but our loving heavenly Father allows us to go. He allows it that we might know Him more intimately as we draw close to Him in the trial and hold on to His hand as He leads us through.

Disappointments will come, contradictions in life will come, and sacrifice will be required. In a difficult time in my own life, one of my journal entries read:

> I feel sliced, pushed back to the second floor, the ceiling is within my reach but out of my grasp.... My heart is wrenched and broken, my stomach aches, and my spirit is cast down. The Lord lifts me up through His Word and the life of Rizpah... My emotions are steady one moment, dull the next, and in dismay, and then devastation the next. I have no recourse but to get hold of myself and my God. I am a servant and I am forever grateful to a gracious God for that.... I cannot let my spirit be tainted by my disappointments... I refuse to get weird through this disappointment. After all, "why are you cast down, O my soul?" Hope thou in God! as the psalmist says. I have much to rejoice in. I will work through this... It's confusing. It's hurtful. It's painful. Perhaps it is yet another way to personally identify with my amazing Savior. All things really do work together for good— for change and growth into His Image—to those who love Him and are called according to His purposes. Keep me, O Lord, in the center of Your will. I love You. I trust You. I choose to rest in You.... I surrender all....

Have you ever felt this way in the middle of a difficult season? The struggle to defend yourself, fight, or react to circumstances rather than respond to the Lord is strong. But surrender to the Lord is what is required. The choice to surrender is what brings ultimate peace and releases faith that is invincible.

If you can't change the circumstances, do yourself an emotional and spiritual favor and change the way you respond to them. If you don't, you will eventually break down instead of breaking through—no treasures will be seen and no hidden riches will be discovered. When you find yourself continually struggling to respond in faith to your circumstances, ask yourself, *Where is my faith?* Is it in the storm or in the Master of the storm? Also ask yourself, *What am I afraid of?* Sometimes we react negatively because we are fearful. Fear is simply faith in the wrong thing; it is misplaced faith. So, if you can discern your fear, you might be able to discern where your faith has gone.

As you respond to the Lord and cease to resist the working of His Holy Spirit in you in the midst of the trial, you will discover the hidden riches. In fact, "Your surrendered need turns into His unlimited opportunity, and He becomes great through you." [26] That's good news! Surrendering to God and trusting Him is the most beneficial thing you can do in the midst of unbendable situations, as God is the God of the unbendable.

Most people have made sacrifices that they have wondered about in retrospect. They wonder if the sacrifice ever really mattered to the Lord or if He ever really took notice of it. What sacrifices have you made that you long to know if the Lord has seen and cared about?

+ Have you served others without appreciation on the job or in the home?

+ Have you tried to be desirable and yet go unnoticed by your spouse?

+ Have you been faithful in the face of marital infidelity?

+ Have you sacrificed your own education and dreams in the reality of ungrateful children?

+ Have you given tithes and offerings to the poor faithfully and yet remained in financial need while others around you who prosper look at you with disdain?

+ Have your heartfelt intercessions and private petitions continued in faith in the face of no answers?

+ Have you been faithful to the principles of the Word of God in the face of ridicule?

+ Have you been dedicated and loyal to your employer or pastor only to be criticized or looked over?

No matter what your circumstances or your sacrifice, there is always hope. Job 14:7–9 says, "For there is hope for a tree, if it is cut down, that it will sprout again, and that its tender shoots will not cease. Though its root may grow old in the earth, and its stump may die in the ground, yet at the scent of water it will bud and bring forth branches like a plant." If your faith has been cut down and the stump is rotting in the ground, the Word of the Lord to you today is that the "scent of water" is near, and at the scent of water you will bud again. Fruit will yet spring forth from your life. The water is representative of the Word of God. I encourage you to stop right now and open up your Bible and read a psalm, a proverb, a blessing in the Word of God. Meditate on Psalm 23 or Psalm 91 if you are unsure where to begin. Let your soul drink in the Word of God and be revived once again. Let your faith blossom in the sunshine of His genuine love for you.

What about the generation following you?

You must live for something beyond yourself. You must live for those who have gone before you and those who are coming behind. That's what the sacrifices of those mentioned in Hebrews 11 accomplished. They did it for us! They did it for our admonition, for our example, for our learning. First Corinthians 10:11–13 says:

> Now all these things happened to them as examples, and they were written for our admonition, upon whom the ends of the ages have come. Therefore let him who thinks he stands take

heed lest he fall. No temptation has overtaken you except such as is common to man; but God is faithful, who will not allow you to be tempted beyond what you are able, but with the temptation will also make the way of escape that you may be able to bear it.

You do not live to yourself—none of us do. Whether you live alone or not, we all live in connection with humanity in some way. There's always someone watching your life whether you realize it or not. When we examine the information given about individual people in the New Testament, we always learn about them in terms of their relationship to someone or something else. For example, Simon was from Cyrene (Mark 15:21), Naaman was a Syrian (Luke 4:27), the woman asking Jesus about her demonized daughter was a Canaanite (Matthew 15:21), Paul was a Jew born in Tarsus of Cilcia (Acts 22:2). When it came to family clans, Mary was of the house of David (Luke 1:27), Zachariah was of the division of Abijah (Luke1:5), Elizabeth was a daughter of Aaron (Luke 1:5), and Paul was of the tribe of Benjamin (Philippians 3:5). [27]

While salvation is personal and can only be realized on an individual level, it is not individualistic to be a follower of Christ. An individual's salvation is not the final goal of God's salvation through Christ. According to Paul, the force of the gospel is to be found in how "the many" (Jews, Greeks, slaves, freemen) became one within the body of Christ. First Corinthians 12:12 says, "For as the body is one and has many members, but all the members of that one body, being many, are one body, so also is Christ." Even though you may sacrifice alone, suffer alone, remain on the Rock alone, you are not alone. There is "a great cloud of witnesses," according to Hebrews 12 that is cheering you on. Like them, you also must live for someone beyond yourself.

If you don't live for something or someone beyond yourself, your vision will be shortsighted, and no long lasting or eternal purposes will be gained. When you experience a personal death of a vision, you must be willing to make that sacrifice for the sake of the greater cause, the generation looking on. You must be willing to make personal sacrifices and lay down your personal hope and dreams, for His will is always accomplished through the avenue of genuine humility. Humility releases faith that is undeniably undefeatable because its foundation is trust in Almighty God.

Although you are allowing yourself to grieve the loss and watch over those precious dreams that you hold dear, you must not retaliate with the arm of the flesh when others toss them aside carelessly. You must not lobby for your own cause or the truths you hold to be personally precious. Neither should you lower yourself to the loathsome depths of gossip or bitterness. You must remain on the Rock, Christ Jesus, in a posture of surrender and humility so that times of healing and refreshing will come from the Presence of the Lord—not for your sake alone, but for the future and hope of others as well. If what you believe is indeed truth and your sacrifice is pure, it will bear fruit that will remain. If you allow the Master to rein in you, the rain of refreshing will come. The sacrifices you offer upon the Rock today will be stepping stones for a grateful generation to come, and great shall be your reward.

Whatever you go through, God is always aware, always watching, and always mindful. Even you cannot feel His Presence, He is closer than you can imagine. He will never leave you or forsake you; you can count on that.[28] What is your destiny? Are you a fire-tipped arrow or has something put out your fire? What is your heritage? Who has marked you? Does that limitation need to be lifted off of you? Where is your hope—on a cross on a hill or in the living Christ?

If you're in a time of contradiction, personal tragedy, or crisis, Jesus wants to minister to you in this moment. If you're in need of strength to remain on the Rock, Jesus wants to give you that strength right now here in His Presence. If you've remained on the Rock, but you've lost sight of purpose and vision, even hope, Jesus also wants to come and encourage and strengthen you in this moment. Reach out in faith for that which you cannot see with the natural eye but is within the grasp of your hope in the future.

A story came to me from an anonymous source that is the frosting on the cake of faith. I believe it to be a true story. It tells of a woman whose heart has been knit across the generations with Rizpah's in faith.

There was a woman who had been diagnosed with cancer and had been given three months to live. Her doctor said she should start making preparations to die.

She contacted the pastor and asked him to come over to her house to discuss certain aspects of her final wishes. She told him which songs she wanted sung at the service, what Scriptures she would like read, and even what she wanted to be wearing. The woman also told her pastor that she wanted to be buried with her favorite Bible.

Everything was in order and the pastor was preparing to leave when the woman suddenly remembered something very important to her. "There's one more thing," she said excitedly. "What's that?" asked the pastor. "This is very important," the woman continued. "I want to be buried with a fork in my right hand." The pastor stood looking at the woman not knowing quite what to say. "That shocks you doesn't it?" the woman asked. "Well, to be honest, I'm puzzled by the request," said the pastor.

The woman went on to explain. "In all my years of attending church socials and functions where food was involved (and let's be honest, food is an important part of any church event, spiritual or otherwise) my favorite part was when whoever was clearing away the dishes of the main course would lean over and say you can keep your fork. It was my favorite part because I knew that something better was coming. When they told me to keep my fork, I knew that something great was about to be given to me. It wasn't pudding; it was cake or pie, something with substance. So I just want people to see me there in the casket with a fork in my hand and I want them to wonder "What's with the fork?" Then I want you to tell them; "Something better is coming, so keep your fork too."

The pastor's eyes welled up with tears of joy as he hugged the woman good-bye. He knew this would be one of the last times he would see her before her death. But he also knew that the woman had a better grasp of heaven than he did. She knew that something better was coming.

At the funeral, people were walking by the woman's casket and they saw the pretty dress she was wearing and her favorite Bible and the fork placed in her right hand. Over and over the pastor heard the question, "What's with the fork?" And over and over he smiled.

During his message, the pastor told the people of the conversation he had with the woman shortly before she died. He also told them about the fork and about what it symbolized to her. The pastor told the people how he could not stop thinking about the fork and told them that they probably would not be able to stop thinking about it either. He was right. So the next time you reach down for your fork, let it remind you, oh so gently, that there is something better coming.

"Now faith is the substance of things hoped for, the evidence of things not seen." [29] It is that which sees further than the past and beyond the present. It is that which believes that "there is something better coming." *Selah.*

God has amazing plans for you today and tomorrow. Whether the "better" of tomorrow is cheery or challenging, it welcomes you to walk the walk of faith and enjoy the journey. Go now—let go of the past, live in the present, and reach for the future in absolute undefeatable faith. God is on your side!

NOTES

1   Kathryn Kuhlman, *I Believe in Miracles* (Old Tappan, NJ: Spire Books, 1969), 10–1.

2   Wendell Smith, *Great Faith* (Portland, OR: City Bible Publishing, 2001), 62–3.

3   Charles S. Price, *The Real Faith* (Plainfield, NJ: Logos International 1940), 53–4.

4   Ibid.

5   Kathryn Kuhlman, *I Believe in Miracles*, 217, 219.

6   Wendell Smith, *Great Faith,* 60

7   Tim Hansel, *You Gotta Keep Dancin'* (Colorado Springs, CO: Victor Cook Communications, 1985), 42.

8   Bob George, *Faith that Pleases God* (Eugene, OR: Harvest House, 2001), 50.

9   E. M. Bounds, *The Complete Works of E. M. Bounds* (Grand Rapids, MI: Baker Books, 1990), 13–9.

10   Gary Kinnaman, *How to Overcome the Darkness* (Grand Rapids, MI: Chosen Books, 1990), 114.

11   John Bartlett, Justin Kaplan, gen ed., *Bartlett's Familiar Quotations 16th Edition* (New York: Little Brown & Co.).

12   "In the beginning was the Word, and the Word was with God, and the Word was God.... And the Word became flesh and dwelt among us, and we beheld His glory, the glory as of the only begotten of the Father, full of grace and truth." (John 1:1, 14)

13   "That which was from the beginning, which we have heard, which we have seen with our eyes, which we have looked upon, and our hands have handled, concerning the Word of life." (1 John 1:1)

14   "For there are three that bear witness in heaven: the Father, the Word, and the Holy Spirit; and these three are one." (1 John 5:7)

15   Wendell Smith, *Great Faith*, 27.

16   E. M. Bounds, *The Complete Works of E.M. Bounds,* 21.

17   Kathryn Kuhlman, *I Believe in Miracles*, 218.

18   These name definitions come from Lareina Rule, *Name Your Baby* (New York: Bantam Books, 1973), 153.

19   Ibid., 89.

20   Ibid., 172, 184.

21   "How precious also are Your thoughts to me, O God! How great is the sum of them! If I should count them, they would be more in number than the sand" (Psalm 139:17–18). "See, I have inscribed you on the palms of My hands; your walls are continually before Me" (Isaiah 49:16). "We know, brothers, that God not only loves you, but has selected you for a special purpose" (1 Thessalonians 1:4, Phillips). "We are His workmanship" (Ephesians 2:10, 22).

22 "Yes, I have loved you with an everlasting love; therefore with lovingkindness I have drawn you. Again I will build you and you shall be rebuilt." (Jeremiah 31:3–4)

23 "He will rejoice over you with gladness, He will quiet you with His love, He will rejoice over you with singing" (Zephaniah 3:17). "For the LORD takes pleasure in His people; He will beautify the humble with salvation" (Psalm 149:4).

24 "We know that, brothers, God not only loves you, but has selected you for a special purpose" (1 Thessalonians 1:4, Phillips). "We are His workmanship" (Ephesians 2:10, 22).

25 "I want you to realize that God has been made rich because we who are Christ's have been give to Him!" (Ephesians 1:17–23, TLB)

26 Bruce Wilkinson, *The Prayer of Jabez* (Sisters, OR: Multnomah Publishers, 2000), 49.

27 Research adapted from a message given by Danny Jenkins at Portland Bible College in 2001.

28 "For He Himself has said, 'I will never leave you nor forsake you.'" (Hebrews 13:5)

29 Hebrews 11:1.

Bibliography

Allender, Dr. Dan B., and Longman III, Dr. Tremper. *The Cry of the Soul: How our Emotions Reveal our Deepest Questions about God.* Colorado Springs, CO: NavPress, 1994.

Bartlett, John, Daplan, Justin, gen. ed., *Bartlett's Familiar Quotations, Sixteenth Edition.* New York: Little Brown & Co., 1992.

Bounds, E. M.. *The Complete Works of E. M. Bounds on Prayer.* Grand Rapids, MI: Baker Books, 1990.

Brenneman, Helen Good. *Meditations for the Expectant Mother.* Scottdale, PA: Herald Press, 1973.
———. Meditations for the New Mother. Scottdale, PA: Herald Press, 1973.

Conner, Kevin, and Kenneth P. Malmin. *Old Testament Survey,* rev. ed. Portland, OR: City Bible Publishing, formerly Bible Temple Publishing, 1975.

Cowman, L. B., ed. James Reimann. *Streams in the Desert: 266 Daily Devotional Readings.* Grand Rapids, MI: Zondervan, 1997.

Damazio, Frank. *From Barrenness to Fruitfulness.* Ventura, CA: Regal Books, 1998.

Easton Dictionary, Bible Works, 5.0, LLC, Software for Biblical Exegesis & Research, Version 5.0.020w, 2001.

Fausset's Bible Dictionary; Bible Works, 5.0, L.L.C, Software for Biblical Exegesis & Research, Version 5.0.020w., 2001.

Freeman, James M. *Manners and Customs of the Bible.* Plainfield, NJ: Logos International, 1972.

George, Bob. *Faith that Pleases God.* Eugene, OR: Harvest House, 2001.

Gill, John. *John Gill's Exposition of the Entire Bible; e-Sword 7.0,* the Sword of the Lord with an electronic edge, 2001.

Grant, Evangelist W. V., *Nuggets in a Nutshell,* Grant's Faith clinic; P.O. Box 353, Dallas 21, Texas, (1950s, no specific date given.)

Grant, W. V. *Growing Faith, Book Three of Divine Healing Answers (Vol. 1),* Dallas, Texas, P.O. Box 353, Dallas, Texas, (1950s, no specific date given.)

Hansel, Tim. *You Gotta Keep Dancin'.* Colorado Springs, CO: Victor, Cook Communications, 1985.

Hitchcock Bible Names, e-Sword 7.0, the Sword of the Lord with an electronic edge, 2001.

International Standard Bible Encyclopedia, Bible Works 5.0, LLC, Software for Biblical Exegesis & Research, Version 5.0.020w, 2001.

International Standard Bible Encyclopedia, e-Sword 7.0, the Sword of the Lord with an electronic edge, 2001.

James, John W., and Cherry, Frank. *The Grief Recovery Handbook: A Step-by-Step Program for Moving Beyond Loss.* New York: Harper & Row, 1988.

Keil and Delitzsch Commentary on the Old Testament; e-Sword 7.0, the Sword of the Lord with an electronic edge, 2001.

Kinnaman, Gary. *How to Overcome the Darkness.* Grand Rapids, MI: Chosen Books, 1990.

Kuhlman, Kathryn. *I Believe in Miracles.* Old Tappan, NJ: Spire Books, 1969.

Lewis, C. S. *The Problem of Pain.* New York: Macmillan, 1962.

Malmin, Glenda. *The Hidden Power of a Surrendered Life.* Portland, OR: City Bible Publishing, 2002.
———. *Woman, You are Called and Anointed.* Portland, OR: City Bible Publishing, 1998.

Meyer, Joyce. *Life in the Word.* New York: Warner Books, 1998.

Oliver, Gary J., PhD, and Wright, H. Norman. *Good Women Get Angry: A Woman's Guide to Handling Anger, Depression, Anxiety and Stress.* Ann Arbor, MI: Servant Publications, 1995.

Peck, M. Scott. *The Road Less Traveled.* New York: Simon & Schuster, 1978.

Peterson, Eugene. *The Message//Remix, The Bible in Contemporary Language.* Colorado Springs, CO: NavPress, 2003.

Price, Charles S. *The Real Faith.* Plainfield, NJ: Logos International, 1940.

Rule, Lareina. *Name Your Baby.* New York: Bantam Books, 1973.

Smith, Wendell. *Great Faith, Making God Big.* Portland, OR: City Bible Publishing, 2001.

Smith, William, rev and ed by F. N. and M. A. Peloubet. *A Dictionary of the Bible.* Nashville, TN: Thomas Nelson 1813–1893.

Strobel, Lee. *The Case for Faith.* Grand Rapids, MI: Zondervan, 2000.

Strong, James, STD, LLD. *Strong's Exhaustive Concordance, Compact Edition.* Grand Rapids, MI: Baker Book House, 1977.

Strong's Concordance, Bible Works 5.0, LLC, Software for Biblical Exegesis & Research, Version 5.0.020w, 2001.

Tenney, Merrill C., gen ed. *The Zondervan Pictorial Encyclopedia of the Bible (Vol. 2, D—G).* Grand Rapids, MI: Zondervan, 1977.

Unger, Merrill F. *Unger's Bible Dictionary.* Chicago, IL: Moody Press, 1966.

Vos, Howard F. *Nelson's New Illustrated Bible Manners and Customs.* Nashville, TN: Thomas Nelson, 1999.

Webster, e-Sword 7.0, the Sword of the Lord with an electronic edge, 2001.

Wilkinson, Bruce. *The Prayer of Jabez.* Sisters, OR: Multnomah Publishers, 2000.

Yancey, Philip. *Disappointment with God: Three Questions No One Asks Aloud.* Grand Rapids, MI: Zondervan, 1988.